Psilocybin Mushrooms; Microdosing; Health and Science.

By Darren Lyman

Hey There and Welcome!

There are many facts and scientific proofs provided and cited within this book.

All opinions expressed are my own and do not represent the Lyman Support Centers or any other project that I am a part of in anyway. Thanks for reading and sharing;

Psilocybin Mushrooms; Microdosing; Health and Science.

by Darren Lyman

800 W. 8th Ave. #110 Denver CO 80204

Text or Call (303) 591-1960 for hours

Table Of Contents

About The Author:

Darren Lyman is a Denver-based entrepreneur with significant involvement in both the cryptocurrency sector and Colorado's burgeoning psilocybin industry. His efforts highlight a unique intersection of technology, alternative medicine, and harm reduction services.

Cryptocurrency Involvement in Denver

Darren Lyman has been an active participant in Denver's blockchain and cryptocurrency community. Known for his passion for blockchain technology, gaming, and live music, Lyman has engaged with local initiatives aimed at promoting innovation within the cryptocurrency space. His work has contributed to Denver's reputation as a hub for blockchain and crypto enthusiasts, aligning with the city's broader efforts to embrace decentralized technologies. Lyman has also been involved in fostering educational opportunities and advocating for blockchain's potential to revolutionize various industries.

Psilocybin Support Center in Denver

After the passage of Proposition 122 in Colorado, which decriminalized psilocybin mushrooms for adults 21 and older, Darren Lyman transitioned into the emerging psilocybin support services industry. He founded a psilocybin support center in Denver, located at 800 West Eighth Avenue #110. The center offers educational sessions and harm reduction support for individuals interested in exploring psilocybin.

In accordance with state law, Lyman provides psilocybin mushrooms free of charge during these sessions, ensuring compliance with regulations that prohibit the commercial sale of psilocybin. Instead, clients pay for the support and guidance provided during their experiences, which include education on safe usage, dosing, and psychological preparation.

Lyman's goal is to create a safe and supportive environment for psilocybin support, offering individuals the tools to navigate their experiences responsibly. He emphasizes the importance of harm reduction principles, aligning with the intent of Proposition 122 to minimize risks associated with psilocybin use.

Legal and Community Response

Darren Lyman's work has not gone unnoticed by local authorities. Denver District Attorney Beth McCann has acknowledged that his business model operates within a legal gray area, as the regulated framework for psilocybin healing centers is still under development. While Lyman's center complies with current state laws by not selling psilocybin, its operations have prompted discussions about how harm reduction services should be regulated and monitored.

The psilocybin support center has also sparked interest in the broader community. Advocates praise Lyman's work for advancing harm reduction and providing a safe space for psilocybin exploration, while critics question whether such services should require stricter oversight.

Impact and Vision

Darren Lyman's dual focus on cryptocurrency and psilocybin support reflects Denver's evolving identity as a hub for innovation and alternative industries. His contributions to both fields highlight a vision for community-oriented entrepreneurship, where technology and wellness intersect.

In the psilocybin space, Lyman continues to advocate for responsible use and public education. By offering harm reduction services and fostering dialogue around psychedelics, he is helping shape Colorado's approach to this emerging industry. As regulations around psilocybin evolve, Lyman's work stands as a testament to the importance of balancing innovation with safety and compliance.

Through his efforts, Darren Lyman has positioned himself as a key figure in two transformative movements in Colorado: the adoption of blockchain technology and the integration of psilocybin into a harm reduction and therapeutic framework. His work exemplifies the entrepreneurial spirit driving Denver's growth in unconventional industries.

Lyman Support Centers

The scientific exploration of psilocybin mushrooms, long considered taboo due to their association with recreational drug use, is now undergoing a significant renaissance. Research into psilocybin, the active compound in these mushrooms, is revealing its potential to revolutionize mental health care and enhance societal well-being. Coupled with the emergence of initiatives like Lyman Support Centers—spaces designed to integrate psychedelic therapies into broader aspects of human society—the future of psilocybin mushrooms appears to hold transformative benefits.

The Scientific Promise of Psilocybin

Psilocybin mushrooms have been used for centuries in spiritual and healing practices. Today, modern science is catching up, and clinical studies suggest that psilocybin has profound therapeutic effects on various mental health conditions. These include depression, anxiety, post-traumatic stress disorder (PTSD), and addiction.

Research conducted at institutions like Johns Hopkins University has demonstrated that psilocybin-assisted therapy can produce rapid and lasting improvements in mental health, even for individuals who have not responded to traditional treatments. In controlled environments, participants report significant reductions in symptoms, coupled with a sense of personal insight, interconnectedness, and emotional healing.

Beyond mental health, psilocybin is also being explored for its ability to enhance creativity, problem-solving skills, and overall well-being. Its capacity to foster introspection and break rigid thought patterns could be instrumental in addressing societal issues like polarization and a lack of collective empathy.

Lyman Support Centers: A New Frontier

As the therapeutic potential of psilocybin becomes more widely acknowledged, structures like Lyman Support Centers are poised to play a pivotal role in integrating these benefits into society. Lyman Support Centers aims to provide safe, supportive environments for individuals undergoing psilocybin-assisted therapy, as well as to foster education and community engagement around psychedelic healing.

Lyman Support Centers are envisioned as multi-functional hubs that combine clinical settings with holistic approaches to mental and emotional health. Key features of these centers may include:

- **Therapeutic Spaces**: Professionals providing support and guidance.
- **Educational Resources**: Education, pamphlets, workshops and seminars on psilocybin's uses, risks, and benefits can help dispel myths and reduce stigma.
- **Community Integration**: The centers can host community events, group therapy sessions, support groups, and encouraging open dialogue about mental health and healing.

By encouraging and normalizing psilocybin use in structured, supportive environments, Lyman Support Centers have the potential to demystify psychedelics and make their benefits accessible to diverse populations.

Societal Benefits of Psilocybin Integration

The societal implications of widespread psilocybin therapy could be profound. As mental health challenges continue to escalate globally, psilocybin offers a novel approach to alleviating human suffering and fostering resilience. Here are a few ways it could reshape society:

1. **Improved Mental Health Outcomes**: With access to psilocybin therapy through centers like Lyman Support, individuals could experience reduced rates of depression, anxiety, and substance abuse, ultimately leading to healthier communities.

2. **Enhanced Creativity and Problem-Solving**: Psilocybin's ability to foster divergent thinking and creative problem-solving could have applications in fields such as education, technology, and the arts.

3. **Greater Social Cohesion**: By promoting empathy and interconnectedness, psilocybin use might help bridge divides, reduce conflict, and cultivate a more compassionate society.

4. **Reduced Healthcare Costs**: Addressing mental health issues more effectively could alleviate the financial strain on healthcare systems worldwide.

5. **Cultural Evolution**: The integration of psilocybin into societal frameworks could spark a broader cultural shift toward valuing mental health, mindfulness, and holistic well-being.

Challenges and Ethical Considerations

While the potential benefits are immense, the road to widespread psilocybin integration is not without challenges. Regulatory hurdles, the need for rigorous scientific validation, and concerns about misuse must all be addressed. Furthermore, ensuring equitable access to psilocybin therapy, particularly for marginalized communities, will be critical in preventing disparities in mental health care.

Ethical considerations also come into play. As the commercialization of psychedelics accelerates, there is a risk of commodifying these substances at the expense of their cultural and spiritual roots. Lyman Support Centers and similar initiatives must prioritize respect for the indigenous knowledge and traditions that have long recognized the power of psilocybin.

A Vision for the Future

The integration of psilocybin mushrooms into society through frameworks like Lyman Support Centers represents a paradigm shift in how we approach mental health and well-being. By combining cutting-edge science with compassionate care, these centers could serve as beacons of hope for individuals and communities alike.

As we navigate the complexities of modern life, psilocybin mushrooms offer a reminder of the profound healing potential that lies within nature. With careful stewardship, their benefits could extend far beyond the therapeutic realm, inspiring a more connected, creative, and compassionate human society. The future, enriched by psilocybin and the support of visionary initiatives, looks promising indeed.

Lyman Support Centers (LSC) stands as a beacon of hope and innovation, fostering transformative partnerships with diverse communities and forward-thinking businesses to integrate psilocybin support into their local ecosystems. By working hand-in-hand with these groups, LSC creates tailored programs that honor cultural individuality while promoting holistic wellness. Their collaborative approach not only inspires those they serve but also sets a powerful example of what can be achieved through unity and shared vision. Together, they are breaking barriers, sparking meaningful conversations, and encouraging others to join in creating a brighter future where mental health and personal growth are prioritized. Through these partnerships, LSC demonstrates the strength of collaboration, inviting more communities and businesses to come together and reimagine the potential for healing and connection.

Visit Lyman Support Centers in Denver Colorado at:

800 W. 8th Ave. #110 Denver Colorado 80204

Call or text (303) 591-1960 for hours.

Harm Reduction

The Lyman Support Center's Approach

The concept of harm reduction is central to Colorado's psilocybin policy and the operations of the Lyman Support Centers in Denver. Harm reduction prioritizes safety, education, and support over punitive measures, aiming to minimize the potential risks associated with psilocybin use while promoting its therapeutic benefits. Darren Lyman's center embodies these principles, offering services that empower individuals to engage with psilocybin responsibly and safely.

Understanding Harm Reduction

Harm reduction in the context of psilocybin involves strategies to reduce the likelihood of adverse effects during and after use. While psilocybin has shown significant potential for treating mental health conditions such as depression, PTSD, and anxiety, its effects can vary based on individual factors, including mental state, environment, and dosage.

Key harm reduction principles include:

1. **Education**: Providing clear, evidence-based information about psilocybin's effects, risks, and benefits.
2. **Preparation**: Helping individuals understand how to create a supportive mental and physical environment (set and setting).
3. **Support During Use**: Ensuring users have access to guidance or assistance if they experience challenging psychological effects.
4. **Integration**: Helping users process and apply insights gained during their experiences to improve mental and emotional well-being.

Harm Reduction Practices at the Lyman Support Center

The Lyman Support Centers integrates these harm reduction principles into its offerings, focusing on education, preparation, and post-experience integration. These practices create a safe and informed space for psilocybin use while adhering to Colorado's legal framework.

Education on Psilocybin Use

One of the center's primary goals is to educate clients about psilocybin, including its potential benefits and risks. Clients are provided with detailed guidance on topics such as:

- The physiological and psychological effects of psilocybin.
- The importance of mental state (set) and environment (setting) in shaping psychedelic experiences.
- Safe practices for consuming psilocybin, including understanding dosage and recognizing personal limits.

This educational approach empowers clients to make informed decisions and reduces the likelihood of misuse or adverse reactions.

Preparation for Psilocybin Experiences

Preparation is a cornerstone of harm reduction. At the Lyman Support Centers, clients are encouraged to reflect on their intentions for using psilocybin and to prepare mentally and emotionally for their experiences. Staff members help clients establish a supportive setting by offering guidance on:

- Choosing a safe, comfortable location for use.
- Involving trusted individuals who can provide emotional support if needed.
- Identifying personal goals or areas of focus for the experience, which can enhance its therapeutic potential.

Integration Support

Integration is essential for deriving lasting benefits from psilocybin experiences. The Lyman Support Centers provides post-experience support to help clients process and make sense of their experiences. Integration sessions focus on:

- Discussing insights gained during the psilocybin experience.
- Applying these insights to personal growth, relationships, and mental health.
- Identifying resources and tools for ongoing self-improvement and emotional well-being.

This support helps clients avoid feelings of confusion or overwhelm and ensures that the benefits of their experiences extend into their daily lives.

The Role of Legal Harm Reduction Services

The Natural Medicine Health Act explicitly permits harm reduction services, recognizing their importance in fostering safe and responsible psilocybin use. The act allows providers to share psilocybin mushrooms free of charge and to offer support services, provided they do not engage in commercial sales of the substance.

The inclusion of harm reduction in Colorado's legal framework reflects the state's commitment to public health and safety. By allowing services like those offered at the Lyman Support Centers, the state ensures that individuals have access to education and support, reducing the risks associated with unregulated use.

Harm Reduction Beyond the Lyman Support Centers

Lyman Support Centers is part of a broader harm reduction ecosystem in Colorado. Community-based initiatives and organizations contribute to this effort by offering services such as:

- **Psychedelic Peer Support**: Trained volunteers provide emotional support for individuals during or after psychedelic experiences, helping them navigate challenges and process insights.
- **Educational Workshops**: Public workshops and seminars educate individuals about the safe and effective use of psilocybin, emphasizing preparation, integration, and risk mitigation.
- **Access to Resources**: Harm reduction organizations connect individuals with mental health professionals, support groups, and other resources to ensure comprehensive care.

These efforts collectively reduce stigma, promote safety, and enhance the therapeutic potential of psilocybin.

Challenges and Opportunities in Harm Reduction

While harm reduction services like those at the Lyman Support Centers play a critical role in Colorado's psilocybin policy, challenges remain. These include:

1. **Regulatory Uncertainty**:
The lack of a fully developed regulatory framework for psilocybin healing centers creates ambiguity for private harm reduction services. Clearer guidelines are needed to ensure consistency and accountability.

2. **Access and Equity**:
Ensuring that harm reduction services are accessible to all individuals, including those from marginalized or low-income communities, is a pressing concern. Advocates have called for subsidies or sliding-scale pricing to address this issue.

3. **Training and Standards**:

Establishing uniform training standards for harm reduction providers is essential to maintain the quality and safety of these services. This includes certification programs for facilitators and integration specialists.

Despite these challenges, the harm reduction model offers significant opportunities to improve public health, reduce stigma, and advance understanding of psilocybin's therapeutic potential.

Conclusion

Harm reduction is a cornerstone of Colorado's approach to psilocybin, and the Lyman Support Center exemplifies how these principles can be implemented in practice. By focusing on education, preparation, and integration, the center provides a safe and supportive environment for individuals exploring psilocybin. Darren Lyman's work not only aligns with the goals of the Natural Medicine Health Act but also sets a standard for harm reduction services nationwide.

As Colorado continues to refine its regulations and expand access to psilocybin, the practices developed at the Lyman Support Center will likely serve as a model for other initiatives. By prioritizing safety, informed use, and public health, harm reduction services are helping to shape the future of psilocybin policy and practice in Colorado and beyond.

Absence of Physical Dependence

Psilocybin, the psychoactive compound found in certain mushrooms, is widely recognized for its ability to induce profound changes in consciousness and mood. Despite its powerful effects, research consistently shows that psilocybin does not induce physical dependence or withdrawal symptoms, distinguishing it from many other psychoactive substances. This chapter explores the pharmacological and neurological mechanisms underlying this unique property, supported by scientific evidence and its implications for therapeutic applications.

Understanding Physical Dependence

Physical dependence occurs when repeated use of a substance leads to adaptive changes in the brain and body, resulting in withdrawal symptoms upon cessation. Substances like opioids, alcohol, and nicotine cause dependence by altering neurotransmitter systems, leading to tolerance (diminished effects with repeated use) and withdrawal (adverse symptoms when use stops).

Key factors contributing to physical dependence include:

1. Receptor Downregulation: Chronic use can reduce the sensitivity or number of receptors, requiring higher doses for the same effect.

2. Neurotransmitter Imbalances: Altered levels of neurotransmitters like dopamine and serotonin can lead to cravings and withdrawal symptoms.

3. Neuroadaptive Changes: Persistent changes in neural circuits reinforce compulsive use.

Why Psilocybin Does Not Cause Physical Dependence

1. **Unique Pharmacological Profile:** Psilocybin interacts primarily with serotonin (5-HT) receptors, particularly the 5-HT2A subtype.

• 5-HT2A Receptor Agonism: Psilocin, the active metabolite of psilocybin, acts as a partial agonist at 5-HT2A receptors. Unlike substances such as opioids or stimulants that heavily target the dopamine reward system, psilocybin does not produce a significant dopaminergic surge, reducing its addictive potential (Nichols, 2016).

• Minimal Dopamine Release: While psilocybin indirectly influences dopamine pathways, the effect is mild and does not reinforce compulsive behavior or cravings.

2. **Lack of Receptor Downregulation:** Receptor downregulation, a hallmark of substances that induce tolerance and dependence, is minimal with psilocybin.

• 5-HT2A Receptor Regulation: Although repeated use of psilocybin can lead to temporary desensitization of 5-HT2A receptors, these changes are short-lived and resolve within a few days without withdrawal symptoms (Halberstadt & Geyer, 2011).

• Tolerance Mechanism: Tolerance to psilocybin's effects develops rapidly after consecutive use but dissipates quickly, discouraging habitual use and mitigating the risk of physical dependence.

3. **Non-Compulsive Use Patterns:** Psilocybin's effects are intense and introspective, often leading users to naturally space out their experiences.

• Self-Regulated Use: Anecdotal and clinical evidence suggests that most individuals who use psilocybin do so sparingly, as the experiences are often emotionally and cognitively taxing. This pattern contrasts with substances like alcohol or stimulants, which are associated with compulsive, frequent use.

• Therapeutic Context: In clinical settings, psilocybin is administered in controlled environments with extended periods between sessions, further reducing the potential for misuse or dependence.

4. **Absence of Withdrawal Symptoms:** Withdrawal symptoms occur when the body reacts to the absence of a substance it has adapted to. Psilocybin does not cause the neurochemical disruptions necessary to trigger withdrawal.

• Neurotransmitter Stability: Psilocybin does not deplete serotonin or other neurotransmitters; instead, it temporarily alters receptor activity without disrupting baseline levels (Nichols, 2016).

- No Physical Symptoms: Studies and anecdotal reports confirm that discontinuing psilocybin use does not lead to physical or psychological withdrawal symptoms.

Scientific Evidence Supporting the Lack of Physical Dependence

1. Preclinical Studies

- Halberstadt & Geyer (2011): Animal studies show that psilocybin does not produce self-administration behavior, a key indicator of addiction potential. This finding highlights its low risk of reinforcing compulsive use.

- Nichols (2016): Research demonstrates that psilocybin does not significantly affect dopamine pathways in the striatum, reducing its potential for physical dependence.

2. Clinical Trials

- Carhart-Harris et al. (2016): In studies on treatment-resistant depression, participants receiving psilocybin reported no cravings or desire to continue use beyond therapeutic sessions.

- Davis et al. (2020): A clinical trial on major depressive disorder found no evidence of dependence or withdrawal symptoms following psilocybin therapy.

3. Observational Studies

- Johnson et al. (2018): Longitudinal studies on individuals who use psychedelics recreationally indicate that psilocybin use is not associated with dependence or compulsive behaviors. Most users reported infrequent use with no withdrawal symptoms.

Therapeutic Implications

1. **Safety in Clinical Use:** The absence of physical dependence makes psilocybin an attractive option for therapeutic applications. Unlike conventional treatments such as benzodiazepines or SSRIs, psilocybin does not carry the risk of dependency or withdrawal.

• Controlled Dosing: Psilocybin's effects are long-lasting, allowing for infrequent dosing schedules in therapeutic settings.

• Minimal Side Effects: The lack of dependence-related complications reduces the burden on patients and healthcare providers.

2. **Treatment for Substance Use Disorders:** Psilocybin's non-addictive nature and unique effects on the brain make it a promising treatment for addiction.

• Breaking Addictive Cycles: Psilocybin helps individuals confront the underlying emotional and cognitive drivers of addiction, such as trauma and compulsive thought patterns.

• Clinical Evidence: Studies on psilocybin-assisted therapy for alcohol and nicotine addiction have shown significant reductions in substance use, with no risk of replacing one addiction with another (Bogenschutz et al., 2015).

3. **Reduced Stigma and Regulatory Barriers:** The scientific consensus that psilocybin does not cause physical dependence may help reduce societal stigma and regulatory restrictions, paving the way for broader therapeutic use.

Scientific Facts About Psilocybin and Physical Dependence

1. Psilocybin does not target the dopamine reward system. Its primary action on 5-HT2A receptors reduces the potential for addictive behaviors (Nichols, 2016).

2. Tolerance is temporary and resolves quickly. Psilocybin-induced receptor desensitization lasts only a few days, with no withdrawal symptoms (Halberstadt & Geyer, 2011).

3. Psilocybin is not self-administered in animal models. This indicates a low risk of reinforcing compulsive use.

4. No withdrawal symptoms occur upon discontinuation. Psilocybin does not disrupt baseline neurotransmitter levels.

5. Clinical trials confirm the absence of dependence. Participants in psilocybin therapy studies report no cravings or compulsive behaviors.

6.   Non-compulsive use patterns are common. Psilocybin's introspective effects naturally discourage frequent use.

7.   Psilocybin is safe for addiction treatment. Its non-addictive nature makes it an effective tool for addressing substance use disorders.

Conclusion

Psilocybin's lack of physical dependence, combined with its profound therapeutic potential, sets it apart from many other psychoactive substances. By primarily targeting serotonin receptors without significantly affecting dopamine reward pathways, psilocybin avoids the mechanisms that drive addiction. Its non-addictive nature makes it a safe option for therapeutic use, including the treatment of substance use disorders and other mental health conditions. As research continues, psilocybin's unique properties will likely play a pivotal role in reshaping modern psychiatry.

References

1.   Nichols, D. E. (2016). "Psychedelics: Mechanisms of action and therapeutic potential."

2.   Halberstadt, A. L., & Geyer, M. A. (2011). "Serotonergic hallucinogens as translational models relevant to schizophrenia."

3.   Carhart-Harris, R. L., et al. (2016). "Psilocybin with psychological support for treatment-resistant depression: six-month follow-up."

4.   Davis, A. K., et al. (2020). "Effects of psilocybin-assisted therapy on major depressive disorder: A randomized clinical trial."

5.   Johnson, M. W., et al. (2018). "The abuse potential of medical psilocybin according to the 8 factors of the Controlled Substances Act."

6.   Bogenschutz, M. P., et al. (2015). "Psilocybin-assisted treatment for alcohol dependence: A proof-of-concept study."

Concept and Practice of Microdosing

Microdosing psilocybin has gained significant attention in recent years as a potential method for enhancing mental well-being and cognitive performance. This practice involves consuming sub-perceptual doses of psilocybin mushrooms—doses that are too small to produce hallucinogenic effects but may confer subtle psychological or physiological benefits. While much of the evidence supporting microdosing is anecdotal, emerging scientific research provides intriguing insights into its potential benefits and mechanisms of action. This chapter explores the concept, methodology, physiological impacts, and scientific evidence related to microdosing psilocybin mushrooms.

What Is Microdosing?

Microdosing involves consuming small amounts of a psychoactive substance, typically one-tenth to one-twentieth of a full psychedelic dose. For psilocybin mushrooms, this corresponds to approximately 0.1 to 0.3 grams of dried material. Unlike full doses, which induce profound changes in perception and cognition, microdoses are intended to provide subtle effects that enhance everyday functioning without disrupting normal activities.

The concept was popularized by psychologist and author James Fadiman, who outlined structured protocols for microdosing in his book The Psychedelic Explorer's Guide. The practice has since gained traction among professionals, creatives, and individuals seeking alternative treatments for mental health challenges.

The Microdosing Protocol

The most commonly followed protocol for psilocybin microdosing is the Fadiman schedule:

1. Day 1: Take a microdose.

2. Day 2: Observe residual effects.

3. Day 3: Rest, with no dose taken.

4. Day 4: Repeat the cycle.

This schedule is designed to prevent tolerance, as psilocybin's effects can diminish with frequent use due to receptor down regulation. Some individuals, however, adopt alternative schedules based on personal preferences or responses.

Mechanisms of Action in Microdosing

At sub-perceptual doses, psilocybin's effects stem from its active metabolite, psilocin, which interacts with the brain's serotonin system. Key mechanisms include:

1. **5-HT2A Receptor Activation**

Psilocin acts as a partial agonist at serotonin 5-HT2A receptors, which are involved in mood regulation, cognitive flexibility, and neuroplasticity. Low-level stimulation of these receptors may explain the mood-enhancing and cognitive benefits reported by microdosers.

2. **Neuroplasticity**

Studies suggest psilocybin enhances synaptic plasticity by promoting the growth of dendritic spines and neural connections. This effect is particularly pronounced in the prefrontal cortex, a region implicated in executive function and emotional regulation (Ly et al., 2018).

3. **Reduction of Default Mode Network (DMN) Activity**

Psilocybin reduces activity in the DMN, a network associated with self-referential thinking and rumination. Sub-threshold doses may subtly modulate this activity, contributing to improved focus and reduced negative thought patterns (Carhart-Harris et al., 2012).

4. **Neurochemical Balance**

Psilocin influences other neurotransmitter systems, including glutamate and dopamine, which play roles in learning, motivation, and reward processing.

Scientific Benefits of Microdosing Psilocybin

1. Mental Health Improvements

Microdosing is widely reported to alleviate symptoms of depression and anxiety. A study by Polito and Stevenson (2019) found that participants who microdosed reported reduced stress, improved mood, and greater emotional stability over a six-week period.

- Depression: Sub-perceptual doses of psilocybin may act as natural antidepressants by enhancing serotonin signaling and promoting neural plasticity.

- Anxiety: Microdosing reduces hyperactivity in the amygdala, the brain's fear-processing center, leading to greater emotional resilience.

2. Cognitive Enhancement

Microdosers often report enhanced focus, creativity, and problem-solving abilities. A 2018 study published in Frontiers in Psychology found that individuals who microdosed performed better on tasks requiring divergent and convergent thinking—key components of creativity.

3. Stress Reduction

Low doses of psilocybin appear to modulate the hypothalamic-pituitary-adrenal (HPA) axis, reducing stress hormone levels. This effect may explain why many users report feeling calmer and more grounded after microdosing.

4. Improved Social Functioning

Microdosing has been associated with greater empathy and emotional openness. By increasing activity in brain regions linked to social cognition, psilocybin may help improve relationships and reduce feelings of isolation.

Challenges and Risks
1.   Lack of Standardization

One of the primary challenges in microdosing research is the variability in dosing and mushroom potency. The psilocybin content of mushrooms can vary widely depending on the species, growing conditions, and preparation methods.

2.   Potential for Tolerance

Although microdoses are designed to avoid tolerance, repeated use over consecutive days can still lead to diminished effects due to serotonin receptor desensitization.

3.   Placebo Effect

Some studies suggest that the benefits of microdosing may, in part, be attributable to placebo effects. For instance, Szigeti et al. (2021) conducted a randomized controlled trial and found that participants who microdosed reported similar benefits regardless of whether they received active psilocybin or a placebo.

4.   Legal and Ethical Concerns

Psilocybin remains a Schedule I substance in many countries, posing legal risks for individuals and barriers for researchers.

Scientific Facts About Microdosing Psilocybin
1.   Psilocybin's half-life is approximately 2-3 hours. However, its effects can last much longer due to changes in brain connectivity (Hasler et al., 2004).

2.   Sub-perceptual doses do not produce visual distortions or hallucinations. This distinguishes microdosing from full psychedelic experiences.

3.   Microdosing may enhance neurogenesis. Preclinical studies show psilocybin promotes the growth of new neurons and synapses in the hippocampus (Ly et al., 2018).

4.   Psilocybin affects serotonin receptors at doses as low as 0.1 mg. This minimal activation is sufficient to produce physiological effects.

5.   Tolerance builds quickly with frequent use. Spacing doses by at least 48 hours helps maintain effectiveness (Nichols, 2016).

6.   Psilocybin is non-addictive. Unlike many psychiatric medications, it does not induce physical dependence or withdrawal symptoms.

7.   The effects of microdosing are cumulative. Users often report progressive benefits with consistent use over several weeks.

8.   Psilocybin enhances connectivity between brain regions. This effect is observed even at sub-perceptual doses (Carhart-Harris et al., 2012).

9.   Microdosing influences inflammatory markers. Psilocybin reduces pro-inflammatory cytokines, suggesting potential benefits for autoimmune and inflammatory disorders.

10.   Psilocybin's pharmacokinetics vary by individual. Factors such as metabolism, weight, and previous exposure influence its effects.

11.   Microdosing has been practiced informally for decades. Anecdotal reports date back to the 1960s, but formal research only began in the 21st century.

12.   Psilocybin mushrooms contain secondary alkaloids. Compounds like baeocystin and norbaeocystin may enhance or modulate microdosing effects (Repke et al., 1977).

Future Directions in Microdosing Research

Despite the promising results, microdosing remains an under-researched area due to regulatory restrictions and the complexity of studying sub-perceptual effects. Future research should focus on:

1.   **Standardized Dosing Protocols:** Developing consistent dosing guidelines to account for variability in mushroom potency and individual response.

2.   **Long-Term Safety Studies:** Assessing the effects of prolonged microdosing on brain function, mental health, and physical well-being.

3.   **Clinical Trials:** Conducting placebo-controlled studies to distinguish genuine effects from placebo responses.

4. **Exploring Secondary Alkaloids:** Investigating the roles of baeocystin, norbaeocystin, and other compounds in modulating microdosing outcomes.

Conclusion

Microdosing psilocybin offers a unique approach to improving mental health, cognition, and overall well-being. While anecdotal evidence highlights its potential benefits, rigorous scientific research is needed to confirm and expand upon these findings. By elucidating the mechanisms of action, standardizing protocols, and addressing safety concerns, microdosing could become a valuable tool in the field of psychiatry and neuroscience.

References

1. Carhart-Harris, R. L., et al. (2012). "Neural correlates of the psychedelic state as determined by fMRI studies with psilocybin."

2. Ly, C., et al. (2018). "Psychedelics promote structural and functional neural plasticity."

3. Nichols, D. E. (2016). "Psychedelics."

4. Polito, V., & Stevenson, R. J. (2019). "A systematic study of microdosing psychedelics."

5. Szigeti, B., et al. (2021). "Self-blinding citizen science to explore psychedelic microdosing."

Therapeutic Uses

Microdosing psilocybin mushrooms has emerged as a promising strategy for addressing various mental health challenges, enhancing cognitive function, and improving overall well-being. While traditional psychedelic doses have been studied extensively for their therapeutic benefits, microdosing offers a novel approach by utilizing sub-perceptual amounts of psilocybin. This chapter explores the therapeutic applications, mechanisms of action, and scientific evidence supporting the benefits of microdosing psilocybin mushrooms.

What Is Microdosing?

Microdosing involves consuming sub-threshold doses of psilocybin mushrooms, typically 0.1 to 0.3 grams of dried mushrooms, which contain active compounds such as psilocybin and psilocin. These doses are too small to induce full-blown psychedelic experiences but are sufficient to exert subtle yet significant effects on mood, cognition, and physiology.

Unlike traditional psychiatric medications, which often target a single neurotransmitter system, microdosing psilocybin appears to influence a broad range of neurological and psychological processes, making it a versatile therapeutic option.

Therapeutic Benefits of Microdosing Psilocybin

1. **Depression and Mood Disorders:** Psilocybin's potential to alleviate symptoms of depression is well-documented, and microdosing appears to offer similar benefits without the intense psychoactive effects of full doses.

   • Mechanism of Action: Microdosing enhances serotonin receptor activity, particularly at 5-HT2A receptors, which play a critical role in mood regulation. This action promotes neuroplasticity, enabling the brain to form new, healthier neural pathways (Ly et al., 2018).

   • Scientific Evidence: A study by Polito and Stevenson (2019) found that microdosing significantly improved mood and reduced depressive symptoms in participants over a six-week period.

2. **Anxiety Reduction:** Microdosing is reported to reduce anxiety by modulating the brain's fear-processing circuits, particularly the amygdala. This effect can help individuals feel calmer and more resilient in stressful situations.

• Clinical Findings: Research has shown that psilocybin reduces hyperactivity in the amygdala, which is associated with the overexpression of fear and worry. Sub-perceptual doses may help maintain this effect without overwhelming the individual (Carhart-Harris et al., 2012).

3. **Enhanced Focus and Productivity:** Microdosing has been linked to improved focus, task management, and productivity. Users frequently report an enhanced ability to concentrate and complete tasks effectively.

• Mechanism: Psilocybin's interaction with serotonin and dopamine systems enhances prefrontal cortex activity, which is crucial for attention and executive functioning.

• Study Evidence: A study published in Frontiers in Psychology (2018) found that participants who microdosed performed better on tasks requiring creative problem-solving and sustained attention.

4. **Creativity and Innovation:** One of the most widely reported benefits of microdosing is enhanced creativity. Users describe greater fluidity of thought, increased divergent thinking, and improved ability to connect disparate ideas.

• Scientific Insight: Psilocybin promotes functional connectivity between previously segregated brain regions, facilitating novel associations and creative insights (Tagliazucchi et al., 2016).

• Applications: These effects are particularly beneficial for individuals in creative professions, such as artists, writers, and designers.

5. **Treatment of Addiction:** Psilocybin has demonstrated efficacy in treating substance use disorders, and microdosing may offer a less intensive option for individuals seeking to overcome addiction.

• Mechanism: Psilocybin's ability to disrupt rigid patterns of thought and behavior can help individuals break free from addictive cycles. Additionally, its impact on dopamine and serotonin systems helps regulate cravings and reward responses (Bogenschutz et al., 2015).

• Preliminary Evidence: While full-dose studies have shown significant benefits, anecdotal reports suggest that microdosing can support long-term recovery by fostering mindfulness and emotional regulation.

6. **Stress Reduction:** Microdosing psilocybin appears to modulate the hypothalamic-pituitary-adrenal (HPA) axis, which governs the body's stress response. This modulation reduces cortisol levels and helps individuals manage chronic stress more effectively.

• Scientific Findings: Studies in animal models have shown that psilocybin decreases markers of stress and inflammation, suggesting potential benefits for stress-related disorders (Ly et al., 2018).

7. **Emotional Openness and Empathy:** Microdosing enhances emotional sensitivity and empathy, allowing individuals to connect more deeply with others and process their emotions more effectively.

• Clinical Observations: Research has shown that psilocybin increases activity in the brain's emotional processing centers, such as the anterior cingulate cortex and insula, fostering greater emotional awareness and interpersonal understanding (Griffiths et al., 2006).

Scientific Facts Supporting Microdosing Benefits

1.   Psilocybin promotes neuroplasticity. It increases the formation of new synaptic connections, particularly in the prefrontal cortex and hippocampus (Ly et al., 2018).

2.   Microdosing influences brain network connectivity. Functional MRI studies show increased connectivity between brain regions associated with creativity, focus, and emotional regulation (Tagliazucchi et al., 2016).

3.   Psilocybin reduces rumination. This effect is linked to decreased activity in the default mode network, which is overactive in conditions like depression and anxiety (Carhart-Harris et al., 2012).

4.   Microdosing lowers inflammatory markers. Psilocybin has been shown to reduce pro-inflammatory cytokines, suggesting potential benefits for autoimmune and stress-related conditions (Ly et al., 2018).

5.   The therapeutic effects of psilocybin are dose-dependent. Even sub-threshold doses can significantly impact mood and cognition without inducing hallucinations (Nichols, 2016).

6.   Microdosing enhances serotonin receptor function. This improvement is crucial for mood stabilization and cognitive flexibility.

7.   **Psilocybin is non-addictive.** It does not induce physical dependence, and its pharmacological profile contrasts sharply with that of conventional antidepressants (Bogenschutz et al., 2015).

8.   Microdosing may enhance emotional resilience. By modulating fear-processing circuits, it helps individuals respond more adaptively to stress and adversity.

9.   Psilocybin affects sleep architecture. Low doses may improve sleep quality by enhancing serotonin-mediated pathways involved in sleep regulation.

10.   Microdosing supports mindful awareness. Users often report increased mindfulness and a greater ability to remain present in daily activities.

Limitations and Future Directions

While the therapeutic potential of microdosing is promising, it remains a relatively new area of research. Current challenges include:

1.   **Placebo Effects:** Studies like Szigeti et al. (2021) suggest that some benefits of microdosing may stem from placebo responses. Further research is needed to isolate genuine effects.

2.   **Lack of Standardized Protocols:** Variability in mushroom potency and individual responses makes it difficult to establish universal dosing guidelines.

3.   **Long-Term Safety:** While psilocybin has a strong safety profile, the effects of prolonged microdosing are not yet fully understood. Future research should focus

on placebo-controlled trials, long-term studies, and the role of secondary alkaloids in modulating microdosing outcomes.

Conclusion

Microdosing psilocybin mushrooms offers a compelling alternative for addressing a wide range of mental health challenges and enhancing cognitive performance. Its therapeutic benefits, supported by growing scientific evidence, include alleviating depression and anxiety, improving focus and creativity, reducing stress, and fostering emotional openness. As research continues to expand, microdosing may become a valuable tool in psychiatry, neuroscience, and personal development.

References

1.   Ly, C., et al. (2018). "Psychedelics promote structural and functional neural plasticity."

2.   Polito, V., & Stevenson, R. J. (2019). "A systematic study of microdosing psychedelics."

3.   Carhart-Harris, R. L., et al. (2012). "Neural correlates of the psychedelic state as determined by fMRI studies with psilocybin."

4.   Griffiths, R. R., et al. (2006). "Psilocybin can occasion mystical-type experiences having substantial and sustained personal meaning and spiritual significance."

5.   Tagliazucchi, E., et al. (2016). "Increased global brain connectivity under psilocybin."

6.   Bogenschutz, M. P., et al. (2015). "Psilocybin-assisted treatment for alcohol dependence: A proof-of-concept study."

7.   Nichols, D. E. (2016). "Psychedelics: Mechanisms of action and therapeutic potential."

Microdosing Overview

Psilocybin, a naturally occurring compound in several species of mushrooms, has gained significant attention for its potential therapeutic benefits. Found predominantly in Psilocybe species, this psychoactive compound has been used in traditional practices for centuries and has recently been the focus of modern scientific research. Microdosing, the practice of consuming sub-perceptual doses of psilocybin, has emerged as a promising area for therapeutic application. This chapter examines the chemical properties, physiological effects, therapeutic potential, and scientific findings related to psilocybin, highlighting its transformative role in mental health and beyond.

Chemical and Alkaloid Properties of Psilocybin

Psilocybin is a prodrug, meaning it is metabolized in the body to produce its active compound, psilocin. Chemically, psilocybin (4-phosphoryloxy-N,N-dimethyltryptamine) is a tryptamine derivative, structurally similar to serotonin, a neurotransmitter critical for mood and cognition. Psilocin, the dephosphorylated active form, binds to serotonin (5-HT) receptors, particularly 5-HT2A receptors, leading to altered neural activity.

Psilocybin-containing mushrooms also harbor other alkaloids such as baeocystin and norbaeocystin. While these compounds are present in smaller concentrations, they may contribute to the overall psychoactive and therapeutic effects of the mushrooms. Research into these secondary alkaloids is ongoing but suggests potential synergistic effects with psilocybin and psilocin.

Microdosing: Concept and Practice

Microdosing involves consuming doses of psilocybin small enough to avoid full-blown psychedelic effects, typically 0.1 to 0.3 grams of dried mushroom. Proponents of microdosing report subtle improvements in mood, creativity, focus, and overall mental well-being without experiencing hallucinations or significant alterations in consciousness.

Therapeutic Uses of Microdosing Psilocybin

1. **Depression and Anxiety Management:** Psilocybin has demonstrated efficacy in reducing symptoms of depression and anxiety, even at microdoses. A 2020 study published in JAMA Psychiatry showed significant improvements in treatment-resistant depression following psilocybin-assisted therapy. Microdosing may offer similar benefits by modulating serotonin activity over time.

2. **Enhanced Cognitive Function:** Microdosing has been associated with improved problem-solving skills and creativity. A study published in Frontiers in Psychology (2018) observed that participants reported enhanced divergent and convergent thinking, essential for creative tasks.

3. **Stress Reduction:** Sub-perceptual doses of psilocybin may help regulate the hypothalamic-pituitary-adrenal (HPA) axis, reducing the physiological and psychological impacts of chronic stress.

4. **Addiction Treatment:** Psilocybin has shown promise in helping individuals overcome substance use disorders. Studies, such as one published in Neuropharmacology (2019), have highlighted its potential in disrupting addictive behaviors and enhancing introspection.

5. **Emotional Regulation:** Microdosing has been linked to increased emotional openness and empathy, fostering better interpersonal relationships and self-awareness.

Mechanisms of Action
The therapeutic effects of psilocybin are thought to stem from its ability to:

• **Enhance Neuroplasticity**: Psilocybin promotes the growth of new neural connections, particularly in the prefrontal cortex, which is associated with executive function and mood regulation.

• **Reduce Default Mode Network (DMN) Activity**: Overactivity in the DMN is linked to depression and rumination. Psilocybin decreases DMN activity, enabling individuals to break free from negative thought patterns.

• **Increase Serotonin Receptor Activity**: Psilocin's affinity for 5-HT2A receptors plays a pivotal role in its mood-enhancing and cognition-boosting effects.

12 Scientific Facts About Psilocybin

1.   Psilocybin is metabolized into psilocin in the liver. This active compound crosses the blood-brain barrier to exert its effects on serotonin receptors.

2.   Psilocybin mushrooms belong to over 180 species, primarily of the Psilocybe genus.

3.   Psilocybin was first isolated in 1958 by Swiss chemist Albert Hofmann, who also discovered LSD.

4.   Microdosing does not induce hallucinations or significant perceptual changes. This distinguishes it from full-dose psilocybin experiences.

5.   Psilocybin enhances brain connectivity. Functional MRI studies reveal increased synchronization between brain regions.

6.   Psilocybin has a low toxicity profile. The compound is considered safe when used responsibly.

7.   Studies show psilocybin can produce lasting effects on mood and behavior. Even a single dose has been associated with sustained improvements in well-being.

8.   Psilocybin affects neuroinflammation. It reduces inflammation markers in the brain, potentially aiding in neurodegenerative conditions.

9.   The compound is non-addictive. Unlike many psychiatric medications, psilocybin does not induce dependency.

10.   Psilocybin therapy is currently in Phase 3 clinical trials for treatment-resistant depression.

11.   Indigenous cultures have used psilocybin mushrooms for centuries. These practices often involve spiritual and healing rituals.

12.   Legalization and decriminalization efforts are gaining traction globally. Cities like Denver and states like Oregon have decriminalized or approved therapeutic use of psilocybin.

Current Challenges and Future Directions
Despite its therapeutic potential, psilocybin remains a Schedule I substance in many jurisdictions, limiting research and accessibility. The stigma surrounding psychedelics is gradually lifting, but regulatory barriers persist. Future studies must explore long-term effects, optimal dosing strategies, and the role of secondary alkaloids in therapeutic outcomes.

Conclusion
Psilocybin, particularly when microdosed, offers a unique avenue for mental health treatment and personal growth. By modulating serotonin activity, enhancing neuroplasticity, and reducing stress, it holds promise for addressing a wide range of psychological conditions. As scientific understanding deepens, psilocybin may emerge as a cornerstone in the evolution of modern psychiatry. The ongoing shift in public perception and policy will likely shape the accessibility and integration of this remarkable compound into mainstream therapeutic practices.

Sources:

1.   Carhart-Harris, R. L., et al. (2018). "Psilocybin with psychological support for treatment-resistant depression: six-month follow-up." Psychopharmacology.

2.   Barrett, F. S., et al. (2020). "Neural and subjective effects of microdosing psychedelics." Frontiers in Psychology.

3.   Griffiths, R. R., et al. (2006). "Psilocybin can occasion mystical-type experiences having substantial and sustained personal meaning and spiritual significance." Psychopharmacology.

4.   Nichols, D. E. (2016). "Psychedelics." Pharmacological Reviews.

5.   Madsen, M. K., et al. (2019). "Psychedelic effects of psilocybin correlate with serotonin 2A receptor occupancy and plasma psilocin levels." Neuropsychopharmacology.

Anti-Inflammatory Properties

Psilocybin, the active compound in certain psychedelic mushrooms, is well known for its effects on mood and perception. Recent research suggests it also possesses significant anti-inflammatory properties, offering potential therapeutic applications for conditions characterized by chronic inflammation, including neurodegenerative diseases, autoimmune disorders, and psychiatric conditions. This chapter explores the mechanisms underlying psilocybin's anti-inflammatory effects, supporting scientific evidence, and implications for medical research.

Inflammation and Mental Health

Inflammation is the body's natural response to injury or infection, involving the activation of immune cells and the release of cytokines. While acute inflammation is beneficial, chronic inflammation can contribute to a range of health problems, including:

1. **Neurodegenerative Diseases**: Chronic inflammation in the central nervous system is linked to conditions such as Alzheimer's disease, Parkinson's disease, and multiple sclerosis.

2. **Mood Disorders**: Elevated levels of pro-inflammatory cytokines are associated with depression, anxiety, and PTSD (Dantzer et al., 2008).

3. **Autoimmune Diseases**: Conditions such as rheumatoid arthritis and lupus involve dysregulated immune responses and persistent inflammation.

How Psilocybin Reduces Inflammation

1. **Modulation of Serotonin Receptors:** Psilocybin's anti-inflammatory effects are mediated through its active metabolite, psilocin, which interacts with serotonin (5-HT) receptors, particularly the 5-HT2A subtype.

• 5-HT2A Receptor Activation: These receptors are expressed not only in the brain but also in peripheral immune cells, including macrophages and T-cells. Activation of 5-HT2A receptors modulates immune responses, reducing the production of pro-inflammatory cytokines such as interleukin-6 (IL-6) and tumor necrosis factor-alpha (TNF-α) (Nichols, 2016).

• Downstream Effects: This receptor activation suppresses nuclear factor kappa B (NF-κB), a key regulator of inflammation, and promotes the release of anti-inflammatory cytokines like interleukin-10 (IL-10).

2. **Reduction of Microglial Activation:** Microglia are the brain's resident immune cells, which become activated during inflammation. Chronic microglial activation is associated with neurodegenerative diseases and mood disorders.

• Psilocybin's Role: Studies have shown that psilocybin reduces microglial activation, thereby mitigating neuroinflammation. This effect is mediated by serotonin receptor signaling, which modulates microglial activity and prevents the release of inflammatory mediators (Ly et al., 2018).

3. **Regulation of Cortisol Levels:** Chronic stress and dysregulation of the hypothalamic-pituitary-adrenal (HPA) axis lead to elevated cortisol levels, which contribute to inflammation.

• HPA Axis Modulation: Psilocybin normalizes HPA axis activity, reducing cortisol levels and systemic inflammation. This effect is particularly beneficial for stress-related conditions, such as depression and PTSD (Carhart-Harris et al., 2017).

4. **Promotion of Neuroplasticity:** Neuroplasticity, the brain's ability to reorganize itself by forming new neural connections, can counteract the damaging effects of inflammation on neurons.

• BDNF and Synaptic Growth: Psilocybin promotes the release of brain-derived neurotrophic factor (BDNF), which supports neuronal survival and repair. Elevated BDNF levels are associated with reduced neuroinflammation and improved brain function (Ly et al., 2018).

5. **Suppression of Pro-Inflammatory Cytokines:** Psilocybin directly influences the production of cytokines, the signaling molecules that regulate immune responses.

• Reduced IL-6 and TNF-α: Psilocybin decreases levels of IL-6 and TNF-α, which are associated with chronic inflammation and tissue damage.

• Increased IL-10: The drug promotes the release of IL-10, an anti-inflammatory cytokine that helps resolve inflammation and restore immune balance (Nichols, 2016).

Scientific Evidence Supporting Psilocybin's Anti-Inflammatory Properties

1. Preclinical Studies

- Ly et al. (2018): In rodent models, psilocybin reduced neuroinflammation by suppressing microglial activation and decreasing levels of pro-inflammatory cytokines. These effects were associated with improved behavior and cognitive performance.

- Flanagan et al. (2021): Research demonstrated that psilocybin modulates peripheral immune responses, reducing systemic inflammation and improving markers of metabolic health.

2. Human Studies

- Carhart-Harris et al. (2017): In patients with treatment-resistant depression, psilocybin therapy significantly reduced depressive symptoms, which correlated with decreased markers of inflammation.

- Davis et al. (2020): A study on major depressive disorder found that psilocybin's therapeutic effects were accompanied by reductions in inflammatory biomarkers, including IL-6.

3. Cellular Mechanisms

- NF-κB Suppression: Psilocybin inhibits the activation of NF-κB, a transcription factor that drives the production of pro-inflammatory cytokines (Nichols, 2016).

- Serotonin Receptor Signaling: Activation of 5-HT2A receptors modulates immune cell activity, promoting anti-inflammatory pathways and reducing chronic inflammation.

Therapeutic Implications of Psilocybin's Anti-Inflammatory Effects

1. **Neurodegenerative Diseases:** Chronic neuroinflammation is a key driver of neurodegenerative diseases like Alzheimer's and Parkinson's.

• Potential Benefits: By reducing microglial activation and promoting neuroplasticity, psilocybin may slow disease progression and improve cognitive function.

2. **Depression and Anxiety:** Inflammation is increasingly recognized as a contributing factor in mood disorders.

• Anti-Inflammatory Mechanisms: Psilocybin's ability to reduce inflammatory cytokines and normalize immune function supports its rapid antidepressant and anxiolytic effects (Davis et al., 2020).

3. **Autoimmune Disorders:** Autoimmune diseases involve dysregulated immune responses and chronic inflammation.

• Psilocybin's Role: By suppressing pro-inflammatory cytokines and enhancing IL-10 production, psilocybin may help restore immune balance in conditions such as rheumatoid arthritis and lupus.

4. **PTSD:** Chronic stress and trauma activate inflammatory pathways, contributing to the development and persistence of PTSD.

• HPA Axis Regulation: Psilocybin normalizes cortisol levels and reduces neuroinflammation, helping patients process trauma and reduce symptoms.

Scientific Facts About Psilocybin's Anti-Inflammatory Effects

1. Psilocybin reduces pro-inflammatory cytokines. Levels of IL-6 and TNF-α, which contribute to chronic inflammation, are significantly decreased after psilocybin administration (Nichols, 2016).

2. Anti-inflammatory effects are mediated by serotonin receptors. Activation of 5-HT2A receptors on immune cells suppresses inflammatory pathways (Ly et al., 2018).

3. Psilocybin suppresses microglial activation. This reduces neuroinflammation and protects against neuronal damage.

4. Inflammatory biomarkers decrease after psilocybin therapy. Studies in depression and PTSD show reductions in systemic inflammation after treatment (Carhart-Harris et al., 2017).

5.   Psilocybin promotes the release of IL-10. This anti-inflammatory cytokine helps resolve inflammation and restore immune balance.

6.   Neuroplasticity counters inflammation-induced damage. Psilocybin's effects on BDNF and synaptic growth protect neurons from inflammatory damage.

7.   Psilocybin normalizes cortisol levels. This helps mitigate stress-induced inflammation and restore immune homeostasis.

8.   Anti-inflammatory effects contribute to therapeutic outcomes. Reductions in inflammation correlate with improvements in mood, cognition, and emotional regulation (Davis et al., 2020).

Conclusion

Psilocybin's anti-inflammatory properties represent a promising avenue for treating conditions characterized by chronic inflammation, including neurodegenerative diseases, autoimmune disorders, and psychiatric conditions. By modulating serotonin receptors, suppressing pro-inflammatory cytokines, and promoting neuroplasticity, psilocybin addresses both the causes and consequences of inflammation. As research continues, psilocybin's role in reducing inflammation may expand its therapeutic applications and solidify its place in modern medicine.

References

1.   Nichols, D. E. (2016). "Psychedelics: Mechanisms of action and therapeutic potential."

2.   Ly, C., et al. (2018). "Psychedelics promote structural and functional neural plasticity."

3.   Carhart-Harris, R. L., et al. (2017). "Psilocybin with psychological support for treatment-resistant depression: six-month follow-up."

4.   Davis, A. K., et al. (2020). "Effects of psilocybin-assisted therapy on major depressive disorder: A randomized clinical trial."

5.   Flanagan, T. W., et al. (2021). "Psilocybin and immune modulation: Implications for systemic inflammation."

6.   Dantzer, R., et al. (2008). "Inflammation and depression: An integrative review of human and animal studies."

Alkaloid Properties

Psilocybin mushrooms are a group of fungi that produce psilocybin, a potent psychoactive compound with profound effects on the human brain. While psilocybin is the most studied compound in these mushrooms, other alkaloids such as psilocin, baeocystin, and norbaeocystin contribute to their complex pharmacological and therapeutic profiles. This chapter explores the chemical properties, biosynthesis, metabolism, and scientific insights into the alkaloid constituents of psilocybin mushrooms.

Primary Alkaloid: Psilocybin
Chemical Structure and Characteristics

Psilocybin (4-phosphoryloxy-N,N-dimethyltryptamine) is a phosphorylated tryptamine derivative. Structurally, it is similar to serotonin (5-hydroxytryptamine), which allows it to interact with serotonin receptors in the brain. Psilocybin is a prodrug, meaning it is biologically inactive until metabolized into psilocin (4-hydroxy-N,N-dimethyltryptamine), its active form.

- Molecular formula: $C_{12}H_{17}N_2O_4P$

- Molecular weight: 284.25 g/mol

- Water solubility: High, allowing for easy preparation of solutions for ingestion or research.

Psilocybin's Mechanism of Action

Psilocybin exerts its effects after dephosphorylation to psilocin, which acts as a partial agonist at serotonin 5-HT2A receptors. These receptors are concentrated in the prefrontal cortex and are associated with higher-order cognitive functions, emotional regulation, and sensory processing. Psilocin also binds to other serotonin receptor subtypes, including 5-HT1A and 5-HT2C, although their roles are less pronounced.

Studies using functional magnetic resonance imaging (fMRI) have demonstrated that psilocybin alters connectivity between brain regions. Specifically, it reduces activity in the default mode network (DMN), a set of brain regions involved in self-referential thinking and rumination. This reduction is linked to the compound's therapeutic effects in depression and anxiety (Carhart-Harris et al., 2012).

Secondary Alkaloids
In addition to psilocybin and psilocin, psilocybin mushrooms contain other alkaloids, which may enhance or modulate the primary psychoactive effects.

1. Baeocystin
• Chemical Structure: Baeocystin is a monomethyl derivative of psilocybin, with one fewer methyl group on the amine moiety.

• Pharmacology: Baeocystin is believed to be psychoactive, though milder in its effects than psilocin. Limited studies suggest it may play a role in the overall experience of consuming psilocybin mushrooms, possibly contributing to unique subjective effects.

2. Norbaeocystin
• Chemical Structure: Norbaeocystin is a demethylated precursor to baeocystin, making it the simplest tryptamine in the biosynthetic pathway of psilocybin.

• Pharmacology: Its psychoactivity remains uncertain, but it is thought to have synergistic effects with psilocybin and psilocin, contributing to the "entourage effect" observed in whole-mushroom consumption (Repke et al., 1977).

3. Aeruginascin
• Chemical Structure: Aeruginascin is a trimethylated derivative of psilocybin, found in specific species such as Inocybe aeruginascens.

• Effects: Anecdotal evidence suggests aeruginascin may induce feelings of euphoria and relaxation, potentially counterbalancing the intensity of psilocin's effects (Gartz, 1989).

Biosynthesis of Psilocybin and Related Alkaloids
The biosynthesis of psilocybin in mushrooms involves a well-characterized enzymatic pathway:

1. **Tryptophan Decarboxylation**: The amino acid L-tryptophan is converted into tryptamine by the enzyme tryptophan decarboxylase.

2. **N-Methylation**: Tryptamine undergoes methylation by methyltransferase enzymes, producing N-methyltryptamine and N,N-dimethyltryptamine (DMT).

3. **Hydroxylation**: Hydroxylation at the 4-position of the indole ring by a cytochrome P450 enzyme yields 4-hydroxytryptamine derivatives, such as psilocin.

4. **Phosphorylation**: Finally, psilocin is phosphorylated by a kinase enzyme to produce psilocybin.

This pathway is remarkably efficient, allowing mushrooms to accumulate significant quantities of psilocybin, often exceeding 1% of their dry weight in species such as Psilocybe azurescens (Gartz, 1992).

Scientific Facts About Psilocybin and Its Alkaloids

1. Psilocybin's effects are dose-dependent. Low doses result in subtle mood and cognition changes, while high doses induce profound sensory and psychological alterations (Griffiths et al., 2006).

2. Over 200 species of mushrooms produce psilocybin. These are primarily from the Psilocybe genus but also include species from Gymnopilus, Panaeolus, and Copelandia.

3. Psilocybin is metabolized into psilocin in under 30 minutes. This rapid conversion explains the onset of effects within an hour of ingestion (Hasler et al., 2004).

4. Psilocybin alters brain network connectivity. Increased global connectivity under psilocybin correlates with feelings of unity and reduced ego boundaries (Tagliazucchi et al., 2016).

5. Tolerance develops rapidly. Repeated use of psilocybin over consecutive days diminishes its effects due to receptor downregulation (Nichols, 2016).

6. Psilocybin has anti-inflammatory effects. It reduces levels of pro-inflammatory cytokines, suggesting potential for neuroinflammatory conditions (Ly et al., 2018).

7.   Psilocybin's toxicity is extremely low. The LD50 in rats is over 280 mg/kg, which translates to a significantly safe profile for human use.

8.   Psilocybin promotes neurogenesis. Preclinical studies show it enhances the growth of new neurons and synapses in the hippocampus (Ly et al., 2018).

9.   Species such as Psilocybe cubensis contain up to 0.5% psilocybin by dry weight. Variations depend on environmental and genetic factors.

10.   Psilocybin inhibits overactivity in the default mode network. This effect is linked to its therapeutic potential in treating depression and anxiety (Carhart-Harris et al., 2012).

11.   Psilocybin mushrooms also contain minor alkaloids. Compounds such as baeocystin and aeruginascin may modulate the primary effects of psilocin.

12.   Psilocybin's psychoactivity is mediated by serotonin receptors. The compound's partial agonism at 5-HT2A receptors is the primary driver of its subjective effects (Nichols, 2016).

Conclusions and Future Directions

Psilocybin mushrooms are complex organisms with a rich biochemical profile. While psilocybin and psilocin are the primary focus of scientific and therapeutic interest, secondary alkaloids such as baeocystin and aeruginascin highlight the need for further exploration into the synergistic effects of these compounds. Research into their biosynthesis, pharmacology, and therapeutic applications continues to expand, providing insights into the mechanisms underlying their profound effects.

As clinical studies progress, psilocybin mushrooms could redefine mental health treatment, offering novel approaches to depression, anxiety, addiction, and other psychiatric conditions. Future work should focus on understanding the individual and collective contributions of these alkaloids to maximize their therapeutic potential.

References

1.   Carhart-Harris, R. L., et al. (2012). "Neural correlates of the psychedelic state as determined by fMRI studies with psilocybin."

2.   Gartz, J. (1992). "Occurrence and variation of psilocybin, psilocin, and baeocystin in Psilocybe mushrooms."

3.   Griffiths, R. R., et al. (2006). "Psilocybin can occasion mystical-type experiences having substantial and sustained personal meaning and spiritual significance."

4.   Ly, C., et al. (2018). "Psychedelics promote structural and functional neural plasticity."

5.   Nichols, D. E. (2016). "Psychedelics."

6.   Tagliazucchi, E., et al. (2016). "Increased global brain connectivity under psilocybin."

Mechanisms of Action

Psilocybin mushrooms, often referred to as "magic mushrooms," have a profound impact on the brain and body through the activity of their primary psychoactive compounds, psilocybin and its metabolite psilocin. These compounds interact with multiple neurotransmitter systems, resulting in a cascade of neurochemical, electrophysiological, and behavioral effects. This chapter explores the mechanisms of action underlying the effects of psilocybin mushrooms, supported by scientific evidence.

Primary Compounds in Psilocybin Mushrooms
1. **Psilocybin**

   • **Chemical Structure**: Psilocybin is a phosphorylated tryptamine derivative (4-phosphoryloxy-N,N-dimethyltryptamine).

   • **Prodrug Nature**: Psilocybin itself is biologically inactive and must be metabolized into psilocin to exert its effects. This occurs through dephosphorylation by alkaline phosphatase enzymes in the liver and gastrointestinal tract (Hasler et al., 2004).

2. **Psilocin**

   • **Active Form**: Psilocin (4-hydroxy-N,N-dimethyltryptamine) is the active metabolite responsible for the psychoactive effects of psilocybin.

   • **Chemical Properties**: Psilocin is structurally similar to serotonin (5-hydroxytryptamine), allowing it to bind to serotonin receptors in the brain.

Key Mechanisms of Action
1. **Interaction with Serotonin Receptors:** Psilocin acts as a partial agonist at serotonin (5-HT) receptors, particularly 5-HT2A receptors.

   • 5-HT2A Receptors: These receptors are primarily located in the prefrontal cortex and are involved in cognition, perception, and emotional regulation. Activation of 5-HT2A receptors by psilocin leads to increased excitatory neurotransmission and enhanced cortical activity (Nichols, 2016).

• Other Serotonin Receptors: Psilocin also binds to 5-HT1A and 5-HT2C receptors, which contribute to its mood-modulating and anxiolytic effects (Madsen et al., 2019).

Scientific Insight: The binding affinity of psilocin for 5-HT2A receptors is critical for its psychoactive and therapeutic effects. Functional imaging studies have shown that blocking these receptors with antagonists eliminates psilocybin-induced changes in perception and consciousness (Carhart-Harris et al., 2012).

2. **Modulation of the Default Mode Network (DMN):** The default mode network (DMN) is a set of brain regions that become active during self-referential thinking, such as daydreaming, introspection, and rumination.

• Effects of Psilocybin: Psilocybin reduces activity and connectivity within the DMN. This disruption is associated with a decrease in ego-centered thinking and an increased sense of interconnectedness with the environment (Carhart-Harris et al., 2014).

• Therapeutic Implications: Overactivity in the DMN is linked to conditions such as depression and anxiety. By reducing DMN activity, psilocybin allows individuals to break free from repetitive negative thought patterns.

3. **Neuroplasticity and Synaptic Growth:** Psilocybin promotes neuroplasticity—the brain's ability to reorganize itself by forming new neural connections.

• Synaptogenesis: Preclinical studies have shown that psilocybin enhances the growth of dendritic spines, which are critical for synaptic communication and plasticity (Ly et al., 2018).

• Brain-Derived Neurotrophic Factor (BDNF): Psilocybin increases levels of BDNF, a protein that supports the survival and growth of neurons. This may contribute to its antidepressant and anxiolytic effects.

Scientific Insight: Neuroplasticity induced by psilocybin is particularly pronounced in the prefrontal cortex and hippocampus, regions associated with memory, learning, and emotional regulation.

4. **Increased Global Brain Connectivity:** Psilocybin alters the functional connectivity of brain networks, enabling regions that typically do not communicate to interact more freely.

- fMRI Studies: Functional magnetic resonance imaging (fMRI) has revealed that psilocybin increases global connectivity between brain regions, breaking down hierarchical organization (Tagliazucchi et al., 2016).

- Subjective Effects: This enhanced connectivity correlates with feelings of unity, expanded consciousness, and creative thinking.

Therapeutic Implications: Increased connectivity helps individuals break free from rigid thought patterns and fosters new perspectives, which are beneficial in treating mood disorders and addiction.

5. **Glutamate Modulation:** Psilocin influences glutamate, the brain's primary excitatory neurotransmitter, which is critical for learning, memory, and synaptic plasticity.

- Mechanism: Psilocybin increases extracellular glutamate levels in the prefrontal cortex, enhancing neural activity and cognitive flexibility (Muller et al., 2018).

- Role in Therapy: By modulating glutamate, psilocybin may help restore normal neural activity in individuals with depression or PTSD.

6. **Reduction in Inflammation:** Psilocybin has anti-inflammatory effects, which may contribute to its therapeutic benefits for mental health conditions.

- Cytokine Modulation: Psilocybin reduces levels of pro-inflammatory cytokines, such as interleukin-6 (IL-6). This effect may alleviate neuroinflammation, which is implicated in depression and other psychiatric disorders (Ly et al., 2018).

- Potential Applications: These findings suggest that psilocybin could benefit conditions characterized by chronic inflammation, such as autoimmune disorders.

7. **Alterations in Brain Oscillations:** Psilocybin induces changes in brainwave activity, particularly in alpha and gamma oscillations.

   • Alpha Oscillations: Psilocybin decreases alpha wave activity, which is associated with ego dissolution and altered states of consciousness (Muthukumaraswamy et al., 2013).

   • Gamma Oscillations: Increased gamma activity under psilocybin is linked to enhanced cognitive processing and emotional insights.

Scientific Facts About Psilocybin's Mechanisms

1. Psilocin binds to serotonin receptors with high affinity. Its action at 5-HT2A receptors is critical for inducing altered states of consciousness (Nichols, 2016).

2. Psilocybin promotes neuroplasticity. This effect is particularly pronounced in the prefrontal cortex and hippocampus (Ly et al., 2018).

3. Psilocybin reduces DMN activity. This reduction is correlated with ego dissolution and reduced rumination (Carhart-Harris et al., 2014).

4. Psilocybin increases global brain connectivity. Functional imaging studies show enhanced communication between brain regions that typically operate independently (Tagliazucchi et al., 2016).

5. Psilocybin elevates BDNF levels. Higher BDNF levels support neuronal survival, growth, and resilience (Ly et al., 2018).

6. Psilocin increases glutamate levels. This modulation enhances cognitive flexibility and learning (Muller et al., 2018).

7. Psilocybin induces rapid antidepressant effects. These effects are observed within hours of administration and can last for weeks (Carhart-Harris et al., 2016).

8. Psilocybin has anti-inflammatory properties. It reduces pro-inflammatory cytokines implicated in neurodegenerative and psychiatric disorders (Ly et al., 2018).

9. Psilocybin alters brainwave activity. Decreased alpha and increased gamma oscillations are associated with enhanced cognitive and emotional processing (Muthukumaraswamy et al., 2013).

10. Psilocybin does not induce physical dependence. Its pharmacological profile contrasts with that of many traditional psychiatric medications (Nichols, 2016).

Conclusion

The mechanisms of action of psilocybin mushrooms are complex and multifaceted, involving serotonin receptor activity, modulation of brain networks, promotion of neuroplasticity, and anti-inflammatory effects. These mechanisms underpin psilocybin's potential as a therapeutic agent for a wide range of mental health conditions, including depression, anxiety, PTSD, and addiction. Continued research will deepen our understanding of how psilocybin interacts with the brain and guide its integration into modern medicine.

References

1. Carhart-Harris, R. L., et al. (2012). "Neural correlates of the psychedelic state as determined by fMRI studies with psilocybin."

2. Ly, C., et al. (2018). "Psychedelics promote structural and functional neural plasticity."

3. Madsen, M. K., et al. (2019). "Psychedelic effects of psilocybin correlate with serotonin 2A receptor occupancy and plasma psilocin levels."

4. Nichols, D. E. (2016). "Psychedelics: Mechanisms of action and therapeutic potential."

5. Tagliazucchi, E., et al. (2016). "Increased global brain connectivity under psilocybin."

6. Muller, F., et al. (2018). "The therapeutic potential of psilocybin for psychiatric disorders: A review."

7. Muthukumaraswamy, S. D., et al. (2013). "Enhanced alpha power during resting state under psilocybin."

Rapid Antidepressant Effects

Psilocybin, the psychoactive compound in psilocybin mushrooms, has gained significant attention for its ability to induce rapid and sustained antidepressant effects. Unlike traditional antidepressants, which can take weeks or months to show significant benefits, psilocybin often produces noticeable improvements in mood and emotional well-being within hours or days of administration. These effects are attributed to its unique pharmacological properties, ability to promote neuroplasticity, and profound impact on brain connectivity. This chapter explores the mechanisms, clinical evidence, and implications of psilocybin's rapid antidepressant action.

The Need for Rapid Antidepressant Therapies

Depression is a leading cause of disability worldwide, with many patients failing to respond adequately to existing treatments. Traditional antidepressants, such as selective serotonin reuptake inhibitors (SSRIs), often take several weeks to produce effects and are not effective for all patients. Treatment-resistant depression (TRD), in particular, remains a significant challenge, necessitating the development of faster-acting therapies.

Psilocybin represents a breakthrough in this regard, offering rapid symptom relief and sustained benefits for individuals with major depressive disorder (MDD) and TRD.

Mechanisms Underlying Psilocybin's Antidepressant Effects

1. **Activation of Serotonin 5-HT2A Receptors:** Psilocybin is converted into its active metabolite, psilocin, which acts as a partial agonist at serotonin (5-HT) receptors, particularly the 5-HT2A subtype.

• 5-HT2A Receptor Role: These receptors are abundant in the prefrontal cortex, a region implicated in mood regulation and decision-making. Activation of 5-HT2A receptors by psilocin enhances excitatory neurotransmission, promotes emotional regulation, and triggers a cascade of downstream effects critical for antidepressant action (Nichols, 2016).

• **Acute Effects:** This receptor activity produces immediate changes in perception and emotional processing, which can help patients reframe negative thought patterns.

2. **Enhanced Neuroplasticity:** Psilocybin promotes structural and functional changes in the brain that support long-term recovery from depression.

• **Synaptic Growth:** Psilocybin increases the density and size of dendritic spines, the structures on neurons responsible for synaptic connections. These changes are most pronounced in the prefrontal cortex, a key area affected by depression (Ly et al., 2018).

• **BDNF Elevation:** Brain-derived neurotrophic factor (BDNF) levels are significantly elevated following psilocybin administration. BDNF is essential for synaptic plasticity and the formation of new neural pathways (Duman & Monteggia, 2006).

• **Clinical Implication:** Enhanced plasticity allows the brain to reorganize maladaptive neural circuits associated with negative thought patterns and emotional dysregulation.

3. **Modulation of the Default Mode Network (DMN):** The Default Mode Network (DMN) is a set of interconnected brain regions associated with self-referential thinking and rumination. Overactivity in the DMN is a hallmark of depression.

• **DMN Suppression:** Psilocybin reduces DMN activity, particularly in the medial prefrontal cortex (mPFC) and posterior cingulate cortex (PCC). This disruption correlates with ego dissolution, a state where individuals experience a diminished sense of self and reduced rumination (Carhart-Harris et al., 2012).

• **Functional Connectivity:** Psilocybin increases connectivity between the DMN and other networks, such as the salience and task-positive networks, promoting a more flexible and adaptive brain state.

4. **Alterations in Emotional Processing:** Depressed individuals often exhibit a negativity bias, where they disproportionately focus on negative stimuli. Psilocybin shifts emotional processing toward a more balanced and positive perspective.

•   Amygdala Regulation: Psilocybin modulates activity in the amygdala, the brain's fear and emotion center. Reduced hyperactivity in the amygdala correlates with decreased emotional reactivity and improved mood (Roseman et al., 2017).

•   Increased Emotional Openness: Patients often report greater emotional insight and a sense of connection to others, fostering empathy and reducing feelings of isolation.

5. **Glutamate Modulation:** Psilocybin enhances glutamate release in the prefrontal cortex, promoting synaptic plasticity and adaptive neural reorganization.

•   Role of Glutamate: Glutamate is the brain's primary excitatory neurotransmitter and plays a key role in learning, memory, and mood regulation. Elevated glutamate levels under psilocybin facilitate the formation of new neural connections (Muller et al., 2018).

•   NMDA Receptor Activation: Psilocin-induced glutamate release activates NMDA receptors, further enhancing neuroplasticity.

Clinical Evidence of Psilocybin's Rapid Antidepressant Effects

1. Randomized Controlled Trials

•   Davis et al. (2020): A study on patients with major depressive disorder found that a single session of psilocybin therapy produced significant reductions in depressive symptoms, with 71% of participants achieving clinical response within one week.

•   Carhart-Harris et al. (2016): In patients with treatment-resistant depression, psilocybin therapy led to rapid symptom relief, with benefits persisting for up to six months in many cases.

2. **Long-Term Effects:** Psilocybin's effects on depression are not merely transient. Sustained benefits are attributed to the drug's ability to promote enduring changes in brain connectivity and neuroplasticity.

- Roseman et al. (2017): Psilocybin-induced changes in amygdala connectivity were associated with long-term improvements in emotional processing and reduced depressive symptoms.

- Patient Reports: Many patients describe a "reset" effect, where they feel liberated from negative thought patterns and better able to engage with life.

Scientific Facts About Psilocybin's Antidepressant Effects

1. Psilocybin acts within hours. Unlike traditional antidepressants, which take weeks to show effects, psilocybin produces rapid improvements in mood and emotional well-being (Davis et al., 2020).

2. Activation of 5-HT2A receptors is central to its effects. This activation enhances excitatory neurotransmission and emotional processing (Nichols, 2016).

3. Psilocybin increases BDNF levels. Elevated BDNF supports neuroplasticity and the formation of new neural pathways (Ly et al., 2018).

4. Psilocybin suppresses the DMN. This suppression reduces rumination and negative self-referential thinking (Carhart-Harris et al., 2012).

5. Amygdala activity is modulated. Psilocybin decreases hyperactivity in the amygdala, reducing fear responses and emotional reactivity (Roseman et al., 2017).

6. Glutamate release is enhanced. Psilocybin-induced glutamate release promotes synaptic plasticity and neural reorganization (Muller et al., 2018).

7. Effects are sustained. Psilocybin promotes lasting improvements in mood and emotional well-being, with benefits often persisting for months (Carhart-Harris et al., 2016).

8. Emotional openness increases. Patients report greater empathy, insight, and connection to others, reducing feelings of isolation.

Therapeutic Implications

1. **Treatment-Resistant Depression:** Psilocybin offers hope for individuals who have not responded to conventional treatments. Its rapid onset and sustained effects provide a much-needed alternative for this population.

2. **Anxiety and PTSD:** By promoting neuroplasticity and emotional resilience, psilocybin may help patients overcome trauma and reduce symptoms of anxiety disorders.

3. **End-of-Life Care:** Psilocybin has shown promise in alleviating existential distress and depression in patients with terminal illnesses, offering emotional peace and acceptance.

Conclusion

Psilocybin's ability to induce rapid and sustained antidepressant effects represents a paradigm shift in the treatment of depression. By activating serotonin receptors, enhancing neuroplasticity, modulating brain networks, and improving emotional processing, psilocybin addresses the root causes of depression in a way that traditional therapies often cannot. Continued research will further elucidate its mechanisms and expand its therapeutic applications, offering hope to millions suffering from mood disorders.

References

1.   Nichols, D. E. (2016). "Psychedelics: Mechanisms of action and therapeutic potential."

2.   Ly, C., et al. (2018). "Psychedelics promote structural and functional neural plasticity."

3.   Carhart-Harris, R. L., et al. (2012). "Neural correlates of the psychedelic state as determined by fMRI studies with psilocybin."

4.   Carhart-Harris, R. L., et al. (2016). "Psilocybin with psychological support for treatment-resistant depression: six-month follow-up."

5.   Davis, A. K., et al. (2020). "Effects of psilocybin-assisted therapy on major depressive disorder: A randomized clinical trial."

6.   Roseman, L., et al. (2017). "Increased amygdala responses to emotional faces after psilocybin therapy."

7.   Muller, F., et al. (2018). "The therapeutic potential of psilocybin for psychiatric disorders: A review."

8.   Duman, R. S., & Monteggia, L. M. (2006). "A neurotrophic model for stress-related mood disorders."

Interactions with Serotonin Receptors

The psychoactive effects of psilocybin mushrooms are primarily mediated through their interaction with the serotonin (5-hydroxytryptamine, 5-HT) receptor system in the brain. Psilocybin, the precursor molecule, is metabolized into psilocin, which acts as a potent partial agonist at several serotonin receptor subtypes, with particular affinity for the 5-HT2A receptor. This interaction underpins the mushrooms' profound effects on cognition, perception, and emotion, as well as their emerging therapeutic applications. This chapter explores the mechanisms of this interaction, the role of different serotonin receptors, and the broader implications for mental health and neuroscience.

Psilocybin and Psilocin: Serotonin Receptor Interactions
Psilocybin as a Prodrug

Psilocybin (4-phosphoryloxy-N,N-dimethyltryptamine) is biologically inactive until metabolized into psilocin (4-hydroxy-N,N-dimethyltryptamine) via dephosphorylation in the liver and gastrointestinal tract. Psilocin is the active compound that interacts with serotonin receptors in the central nervous system (Hasler et al., 2004).

Psilocin's Structural Similarity to Serotonin

Psilocin closely resembles serotonin in its molecular structure, allowing it to bind to serotonin receptors. This structural mimicry explains psilocin's broad effects on mood, cognition, and perception, as serotonin is a key neurotransmitter involved in these functions.

Key Serotonin Receptors Affected by Psilocin
1. 5-HT2A Receptor

•	Primary Target: The 5-HT2A receptor is the principal mediator of psilocin's psychoactive effects (Nichols, 2016).

- Mechanism of Action: Psilocin acts as a partial agonist at 5-HT2A receptors, inducing conformational changes in the receptor that alter downstream signaling pathways. This activation enhances excitatory neurotransmission and cortical activity, particularly in the prefrontal cortex, which is associated with higher-order cognitive functions and emotional processing.

- Therapeutic Implications: Activation of 5-HT2A receptors is linked to enhanced neuroplasticity, reduced rumination, and improved emotional regulation, making psilocybin a promising treatment for depression, anxiety, and PTSD (Carhart-Harris et al., 2016).

2. 5-HT1A Receptor

- Secondary Target: Psilocin also binds to 5-HT1A receptors, though with lower affinity than 5-HT2A receptors.

- Mechanism of Action: Activation of 5-HT1A receptors is associated with anxiolytic and mood-stabilizing effects. Psilocin's activity at these receptors likely contributes to its calming and emotionally stabilizing properties (Madsen et al., 2019).

3. 5-HT2C Receptor

- Additional Target: Psilocin interacts with 5-HT2C receptors, which are involved in regulating appetite, mood, and anxiety.

- Effects on Emotion: Activity at 5-HT2C receptors may complement the effects of 5-HT2A receptor activation by modulating emotional responses and stress regulation (Nichols, 2016).

Functional Outcomes of Serotonin Receptor Interaction

1. **Enhanced Neurotransmission:** Psilocin's partial agonism at 5-HT2A receptors enhances glutamatergic neurotransmission in the prefrontal cortex. This increased excitatory activity underlies the profound changes in perception, thought patterns, and emotional processing associated with psilocybin use (Muller et al., 2018).

2. **Increased Neuroplasticity:** Activation of 5-HT2A receptors stimulates pathways involved in neuroplasticity, such as the release of brain-derived neurotrophic factor

(BDNF). BDNF supports the growth and survival of neurons, enabling the brain to form new connections and adapt to changes (Ly et al., 2018).

  •   Clinical Relevance: This neuroplasticity is critical for overcoming rigid thought patterns in conditions like depression and anxiety.

3. **Modulation of the Default Mode Network (DMN):** Psilocin's effects on serotonin receptors, particularly 5-HT2A, reduce activity in the DMN, a brain network implicated in self-referential thinking and rumination. This reduction allows for increased brain connectivity and a shift in perspective, often described as a "reset" of the mind (Carhart-Harris et al., 2012).

Scientific Facts about Psilocybin's Interaction with Serotonin Receptors

1.   Psilocin has a high binding affinity for 5-HT2A receptors. This receptor is primarily responsible for its psychoactive effects (Nichols, 2016).

2.   Psilocin acts as a partial agonist. Unlike full agonists, partial agonists like psilocin activate receptors without overstimulating them, resulting in a balanced response.

3.   5-HT2A receptor activation enhances glutamate release. This excitatory neurotransmitter is critical for cognition and neuroplasticity (Muller et al., 2018).

4.   Psilocybin increases brain-derived neurotrophic factor (BDNF). Elevated BDNF levels promote neural growth and synaptic remodeling (Ly et al., 2018).

5.   Psilocybin modulates serotonin receptor activity at sub-perceptual doses. Even microdoses have measurable effects on serotonin receptor activity, contributing to mood and cognitive improvements (Polito & Stevenson, 2019).

6.   Blocking 5-HT2A receptors eliminates psilocybin's effects. This finding confirms the central role of 5-HT2A receptors in mediating psilocybin's psychoactivity (Carhart-Harris et al., 2012).

7.   Psilocybin alters cortical oscillations. Changes in alpha and gamma brainwaves are linked to serotonin receptor activity and altered states of consciousness (Muthukumaraswamy et al., 2013).

8.   5-HT2A receptors are densely located in the prefrontal cortex. This region is responsible for higher-order cognitive processes and emotional regulation.

9.   Psilocin's effects are dose-dependent. Higher doses result in stronger 5-HT2A receptor activation and more profound changes in perception and cognition.

10.   Psilocybin is non-addictive. Unlike many drugs that act on serotonin receptors, psilocybin does not induce dependence or withdrawal symptoms (Nichols, 2016).

Implications for Therapy

1. **Treatment of Depression:** By activating 5-HT2A receptors and promoting neuroplasticity, psilocybin facilitates the reorganization of neural pathways involved in depressive thought patterns (Carhart-Harris et al., 2016).

2. **Reduction of Anxiety:** Psilocybin's interaction with 5-HT1A and 5-HT2A receptors reduces fear responses and enhances emotional resilience, making it effective for treating anxiety disorders (Madsen et al., 2019).

3. **Addiction Treatment:** Psilocybin disrupts maladaptive neural circuits associated with addiction by engaging serotonin receptors and enhancing cognitive flexibility (Bogenschutz et al., 2015).

Conclusion

The interaction of psilocybin mushrooms with serotonin receptors, particularly 5-HT2A, forms the foundation of their psychoactive and therapeutic effects. By modulating serotonin receptor activity, psilocin enhances neurotransmission, promotes neuroplasticity, and alters brain network dynamics. These mechanisms not only explain the profound changes in perception and consciousness induced by psilocybin but also support its therapeutic potential for treating depression, anxiety, and addiction. Continued research into these interactions will deepen our understanding of psilocybin's mechanisms and pave the way for its integration into modern psychiatric treatment.

References

1. Carhart-Harris, R. L., et al. (2012). "Neural correlates of the psychedelic state as determined by fMRI studies with psilocybin."

2. Ly, C., et al. (2018). "Psychedelics promote structural and functional neural plasticity."

3. Madsen, M. K., et al. (2019). "Psychedelic effects of psilocybin correlate with serotonin 2A receptor occupancy and plasma psilocin levels."

4. Muller, F., et al. (2018). "The therapeutic potential of psilocybin for psychiatric disorders: A review."

5. Nichols, D. E. (2016). "Psychedelics: Mechanisms of action and therapeutic potential."

6. Polito, V., & Stevenson, R. J. (2019). "A systematic study of microdosing psychedelics."

7. Muthukumaraswamy, S. D., et al. (2013). "Enhanced alpha power during resting state under psilocybin."

Alters Brainwave Activity

Psilocybin, the active compound in psychedelic mushrooms, induces profound changes in brainwave activity, a key factor underlying its effects on consciousness, cognition, and emotion. Brainwave activity reflects the synchronized electrical oscillations of neurons and plays a fundamental role in how the brain processes information, forms memories, and regulates emotions. Psilocybin's influence on brainwave patterns provides insight into its therapeutic effects, including its ability to disrupt maladaptive thought patterns and enhance neuroplasticity. This chapter explores the mechanisms by which psilocybin alters brainwave activity, its implications for mental health, and the supporting scientific evidence.

Understanding Brainwave Activity

Brainwaves are categorized based on their frequency and are associated with different cognitive and emotional states:

1. Delta Waves (0.5-4 Hz): Dominant during deep sleep and associated with restorative processes.

2. Theta Waves (4-8 Hz): Linked to relaxation, creativity, and introspection.

3. Alpha Waves (8-13 Hz): Associated with calmness and meditative states; prominent during relaxed wakefulness.

4. Beta Waves (13-30 Hz): Involved in active thinking, focus, and problem-solving.

5. Gamma Waves (30-100 Hz): Associated with high-level cognitive processing, such as attention, memory, and sensory perception.

Psilocybin's effects on brainwave activity vary across these frequency bands, disrupting typical patterns and promoting novel neural dynamics.

How Psilocybin Alters Brainwave Activity

1. **Reduction in Alpha Power:** Alpha waves, primarily generated in the posterior cingulate cortex (PCC) and occipital lobe, are associated with self-referential thinking and introspection.

• Alpha Suppression: Psilocybin significantly reduces alpha power, particularly in the Default Mode Network (DMN), disrupting habitual patterns of self-focused thought and facilitating ego dissolution (Muthukumaraswamy et al., 2013).

• Therapeutic Implications: Alpha suppression correlates with reduced rumination and negative thought patterns, key features of depression.

2. **Increase in Gamma Activity:** Gamma waves are the fastest brainwaves and are crucial for information integration and conscious awareness.

• Enhanced Gamma Oscillations: Psilocybin increases gamma power, particularly in the prefrontal cortex and sensory areas. This enhancement is associated with heightened sensory perception, emotional processing, and the vividness of psychedelic experiences (Muthukumaraswamy et al., 2013).

• Neural Synchrony: Elevated gamma activity improves synchronization between brain regions, supporting enhanced connectivity and cognitive flexibility (Tagliazucchi et al., 2016).

3. **Disruption of Default Mode Network (DMN) Oscillations:** The DMN, a network of brain regions involved in self-referential thinking and rumination, exhibits distinct oscillatory patterns under normal conditions.

• Psilocybin's Effect: Psilocybin disrupts the coherence of oscillatory activity within the DMN, reducing its dominance and allowing other networks to take precedence. This effect underlies the experience of ego dissolution and increased focus on the external environment (Carhart-Harris et al., 2012).

4. **Promotion of Theta Activity:** Theta waves are associated with creativity, intuition, and emotional insight.

- Increased Theta Power: Psilocybin enhances theta activity, particularly in the hippocampus and anterior cingulate cortex. This increase facilitates introspection, emotional breakthroughs, and the processing of traumatic memories.

- Applications: Elevated theta activity may explain psilocybin's efficacy in psychotherapy, where patients often report profound emotional insights (Nichols, 2016).

5. **Induction of Fractal Brainwave Dynamics:** Fractal patterns in brainwave activity indicate increased complexity and adaptability of neural networks.

- Fractal Activity Under Psilocybin: Studies suggest that psilocybin induces fractal-like oscillatory dynamics, reflecting a shift toward a more entropic and flexible brain state (Carhart-Harris et al., 2014).

- Implications for Mental Health: Increased entropy allows individuals to escape rigid thought patterns and adopt new perspectives, a key feature of psilocybin's therapeutic effects.

Therapeutic Implications of Brainwave Changes
1. **Depression and Anxiety:** Depression is characterized by hyperconnectivity within the DMN and reduced flexibility in brainwave activity.

- Alpha Suppression and DMN Disruption: Psilocybin's effects on alpha waves and DMN coherence help alleviate depressive symptoms by breaking habitual patterns of negative thought (Carhart-Harris et al., 2016).

- Gamma Enhancement: Elevated gamma activity supports emotional processing and cognitive reappraisal, contributing to sustained mood improvements.

2. **PTSD and Trauma Processing:** Trauma disrupts normal brainwave dynamics, leading to hypervigilance and emotional dysregulation.

- Theta Activity: Psilocybin's enhancement of theta waves facilitates the processing of traumatic memories and emotional healing, making it an effective tool for treating PTSD (Nichols, 2016).

- Integration of Experience: Increased gamma synchrony helps patients integrate their experiences and gain a new perspective on past trauma.

3. **Cognitive Enhancement:** Psilocybin's effects on gamma activity enhance cognitive flexibility and creativity.

• Problem-Solving and Insight: Increased gamma and theta oscillations are associated with improved problem-solving, innovative thinking, and the ability to make novel connections (Tagliazucchi et al., 2016).

• Applications: These changes make psilocybin a promising tool for enhancing creativity and addressing cognitive rigidity in neurodegenerative conditions.

Scientific Evidence Supporting Psilocybin's Effects on Brainwave Activity

1. **Magnetoencephalography (MEG) Studies:** Muthukumaraswamy et al. (2013): MEG recordings revealed significant reductions in alpha power and increased gamma activity following psilocybin administration. These changes correlated with subjective reports of ego dissolution and enhanced sensory perception.

2. **Functional MRI Studies:** Carhart-Harris et al. (2012): fMRI studies showed that psilocybin disrupts DMN activity and alters oscillatory patterns, facilitating a shift from self-focused to externally focused cognition.

3. **EEG Studies:** Tagliazucchi et al. (2016): EEG studies demonstrated increased global connectivity and enhanced neural synchrony under psilocybin, driven by changes in brainwave activity across multiple frequency bands.

Scientific Facts About Psilocybin and Brainwave Activity

1. Psilocybin reduces alpha power in the DMN. This suppression correlates with ego dissolution and reduced rumination (Muthukumaraswamy et al., 2013).

2. Gamma oscillations are enhanced under psilocybin. Elevated gamma activity supports heightened sensory perception and emotional processing (Tagliazucchi et al., 2016).

3. Theta activity is increased in key brain regions. Psilocybin enhances theta waves in the hippocampus and anterior cingulate cortex, facilitating emotional insight and trauma processing.

4.   Fractal brainwave dynamics emerge. Psilocybin induces fractal-like oscillatory patterns, reflecting increased neural entropy and flexibility (Carhart-Harris et al., 2014).

5.   Brainwave changes promote neuroplasticity. Alterations in alpha and gamma activity enhance synaptic plasticity and neural connectivity.

6.   Oscillatory disruption supports therapeutic outcomes. Changes in brainwave patterns correlate with improvements in depression, anxiety, and PTSD symptoms.

7.   Gamma synchrony enhances cognitive flexibility. Psilocybin's effects on gamma activity promote innovative thinking and problem-solving.

8.   Brainwave changes are dose-dependent. Higher doses of psilocybin produce more pronounced alterations in brainwave activity.

Conclusion

Psilocybin induces profound changes in brainwave activity, disrupting maladaptive patterns and promoting greater neural flexibility. By suppressing alpha power, enhancing gamma and theta oscillations, and disrupting DMN coherence, psilocybin facilitates emotional processing, cognitive flexibility, and neuroplasticity. These changes underpin its therapeutic effects for conditions like depression, PTSD, and anxiety. As research continues, understanding the relationship between psilocybin and brainwave activity will further elucidate its mechanisms and expand its applications in neuroscience and mental health treatment.

References

1.   Muthukumaraswamy, S. D., et al. (2013). "Enhanced gamma oscillations and reduced alpha power under psilocybin."

2.   Carhart-Harris, R. L., et al. (2012). "Neural correlates of the psychedelic state as determined by fMRI studies with psilocybin."

3.   Tagliazucchi, E., et al. (2016). "Increased global brain connectivity under psilocybin."

4.   Nichols, D. E. (2016). "Psychedelics: Mechanisms of action and therapeutic potential."

5.   Carhart-Harris, R. L., et al. (2014). "The entropic brain: A theory of conscious states informed by neuroimaging research with psychedelics."

Global Brain Connectivity

Psilocybin, the primary psychoactive compound in psilocybin mushrooms, has been shown to dramatically enhance global brain connectivity. This refers to the increased communication and integration between regions of the brain that typically operate independently. These changes in connectivity are associated with altered states of consciousness, cognitive flexibility, and therapeutic benefits for mental health conditions. This chapter examines how psilocybin affects global brain connectivity, the mechanisms involved, and its implications for psychological well-being and treatment, supported by scientific evidence.

What Is Global Brain Connectivity?

Global brain connectivity describes the extent to which different regions of the brain are interconnected and communicate with one another. It involves two main aspects:

1.   Functional Connectivity: Refers to the temporal correlation of neural activity between brain regions. Strong functional connectivity implies that these regions work together dynamically.

2.   Structural Connectivity: Refers to the physical pathways that link brain regions, such as white matter tracts.

Under normal conditions, the brain operates in specialized, modular networks, such as the default mode network (DMN), salience network, and executive control network. While this modularity supports efficient cognitive functioning, excessive segregation can contribute to rigid thought patterns and mental health issues.

How Psilocybin Enhances Global Brain Connectivity

1. **Disruption of Normal Network Hierarchies:** Psilocybin disrupts the hierarchical organization of the brain, reducing dominance of high-order networks like the DMN and increasing communication between previously segregated regions.

• Scientific Evidence: Carhart-Harris et al. (2014) used functional magnetic resonance imaging (fMRI) to show that psilocybin reduces DMN activity and increases connectivity between the DMN and other networks, such as the salience and sensory networks. This reorganization fosters a more integrated and flexible brain state.

2. **Increased Functional Connectivity:** Psilocybin facilitates a more globally connected brain state, enabling regions that do not typically interact to communicate.

• Dynamic Rewiring: Tagliazucchi et al. (2016) demonstrated that psilocybin significantly increases functional connectivity across cortical and subcortical regions, allowing for the formation of novel neural pathways. This enhanced connectivity correlates with subjective experiences of ego dissolution and heightened creativity.

• Cross-Network Integration: Enhanced connectivity between networks, such as the DMN and task-positive networks, allows for a balance between self-referential thought and external focus, which is often disrupted in depression and anxiety.

3. **Role of Serotonin Receptors:** The increased connectivity observed under psilocybin is mediated by its action on serotonin 5-HT2A receptors, which are abundant in cortical areas involved in higher-order processing.

• 5-HT2A Receptor Activation: Psilocin, the active metabolite of psilocybin, binds to 5-HT2A receptors, enhancing cortical excitability and neuroplasticity. This receptor activation disrupts normal network segregation, enabling regions to communicate more freely (Nichols, 2016).

• Increased Neuroplasticity: Psilocybin promotes synaptogenesis and dendritic growth, which are critical for forming and maintaining new connections between brain regions (Ly et al., 2018).

4. **Alterations in Oscillatory Activity:** Psilocybin induces changes in brainwave patterns, which play a key role in mediating global connectivity.

• Gamma Oscillations: Psilocybin increases gamma activity, which is associated with higher cognitive processes and network integration (Muthukumaraswamy et al., 2013).

- Alpha Suppression: Reduced alpha power in the default mode network facilitates communication with other networks, promoting a more interconnected brain state.

Therapeutic Implications of Increased Global Connectivity

1. **Breaking Rigid Thought Patterns:** Conditions like depression, anxiety, and PTSD are associated with rigid, maladaptive neural circuits. Increased connectivity allows the brain to break free from these loops and adopt more flexible patterns of thinking.

- Depression: Research by Carhart-Harris et al. (2017) found that patients with treatment-resistant depression experienced significant symptom improvement after psilocybin therapy. These benefits were linked to increased global connectivity and reduced segregation of brain networks.

- PTSD: Enhanced connectivity between the amygdala (involved in fear processing) and the prefrontal cortex (involved in emotional regulation) helps patients process traumatic memories in a healthier way.

2. **Ego Dissolution and Emotional Openness:** Psilocybin's ability to increase connectivity between networks that regulate self-referential and sensory processing underlies the phenomenon of ego dissolution, where individuals feel a reduced sense of self and increased unity with their environment.

- Clinical Significance: Ego dissolution allows patients to step outside their usual perspective, fostering greater emotional openness and a more objective view of their thoughts and behaviors (Griffiths et al., 2016).

3. **Enhanced Creativity and Problem-Solving:** By enabling communication between brain regions that typically do not interact, psilocybin enhances creativity and problem-solving abilities.

- Creative Cognition: Increased connectivity between the DMN and task-positive networks facilitates divergent thinking, which is essential for generating novel ideas and solutions (Tagliazucchi et al., 2016).

- Applications: These effects are particularly beneficial for individuals in creative fields or those seeking to overcome mental blocks.

Scientific Evidence Supporting Global Connectivity

1. **Functional Imaging Studies:** Carhart-Harris et al. (2014) used fMRI to show that psilocybin increases global integration of brain activity, particularly between the DMN, salience network, and sensory networks. This enhanced connectivity was associated with subjective reports of ego dissolution and altered consciousness.

2. **Magnetoencephalography (MEG) Studies:** Muthukumaraswamy et al. (2013) demonstrated that psilocybin alters oscillatory activity in the brain, particularly increasing gamma power and reducing alpha power. These changes facilitate greater communication between brain regions.

3. **Long-Term Connectivity Changes:** A study by Roseman et al. (2017) found that psilocybin-induced connectivity changes persisted for weeks after the experience, correlating with long-term improvements in mood and cognition.

Scientific Facts About Psilocybin and Global Brain Connectivity

1. Psilocybin increases connectivity between segregated brain regions. This enhanced integration correlates with subjective experiences of unity and openness (Tagliazucchi et al., 2016).

2. Global connectivity is mediated by 5-HT2A receptor activation. These receptors enhance cortical excitability and disrupt normal network segregation (Nichols, 2016).

3. Psilocybin promotes long-term connectivity changes. These changes support sustained therapeutic benefits, such as reduced depression and anxiety (Roseman et al., 2017).

4. Increased connectivity underlies ego dissolution. Reduced dominance of the DMN allows for a diminished sense of self and increased connection with the environment (Carhart-Harris et al., 2014).

5. Psilocybin alters brain oscillations. Increased gamma and reduced alpha activity facilitate cross-network communication (Muthukumaraswamy et al., 2013).

6.   Enhanced connectivity fosters emotional flexibility. Patients experience greater emotional regulation and reduced fear responses after psilocybin therapy (Griffiths et al., 2016).

7.   Increased connectivity aids creative thinking. Psilocybin promotes divergent thinking by facilitating communication between the DMN and task-positive networks.

Conclusion

Psilocybin mushrooms enhance global brain connectivity by disrupting hierarchical network structures, increasing functional integration, and promoting neuroplasticity. These changes allow for greater communication between previously segregated brain regions, supporting cognitive flexibility, emotional regulation, and creative thinking. This increased connectivity is central to psilocybin's therapeutic effects, enabling individuals to overcome rigid thought patterns and adopt healthier mental states. As research continues, understanding the mechanisms underlying global connectivity will further clarify psilocybin's potential in treating mental health disorders and enhancing human cognition.

References

1.   Carhart-Harris, R. L., et al. (2014). "The entropic brain: A theory of conscious states informed by neuroimaging research with psychedelics."

2.   Tagliazucchi, E., et al. (2016). "Increased global brain connectivity under psilocybin."

3.   Muthukumaraswamy, S. D., et al. (2013). "Enhanced gamma oscillations under psilocybin."

4.   Roseman, L., et al. (2017). "Increased amygdala responses to emotional faces after psilocybin therapy."

5.   Nichols, D. E. (2016). "Psychedelics: Mechanisms of action and therapeutic potential."

6.   Griffiths, R. R., et al. (2016). "Psilocybin produces substantial and sustained decreases in depression and anxiety in patients with life-threatening cancer."

Increasing Neuroplasticity

Neuroplasticity, the brain's ability to reorganize itself by forming new neural connections, is a crucial process for learning, memory, emotional adaptation, and recovery from brain injuries or mental health disorders. Psilocybin, the primary psychoactive compound in psilocybin mushrooms, has been shown to enhance neuroplasticity through mechanisms involving serotonin receptor activation, synaptic growth, and increased brain connectivity. This chapter examines the role of psilocybin in promoting neuroplasticity, supported by scientific evidence and insights.

Neuroplasticity allows the brain to adapt to new experiences, recover from injury, and modify its structure and function in response to changes in the environment. It is particularly important in overcoming mental health challenges, as conditions such as depression, anxiety, and PTSD often involve rigid and maladaptive neural pathways.

How Psilocybin Enhances Neuroplasticity

1. **Activation of Serotonin Receptors:** Psilocybin's neuroplastic effects are primarily mediated through its active metabolite, psilocin, which interacts with serotonin receptors, particularly 5-HT2A.

•	Role of 5-HT2A Receptors: Psilocin acts as a partial agonist at 5-HT2A receptors, which are abundant in brain regions such as the prefrontal cortex and hippocampus. These receptors regulate synaptic transmission, dendritic growth, and plasticity (Nichols, 2016).

•	Downstream Effects: Activation of 5-HT2A receptors triggers intracellular signaling cascades that promote the release of brain-derived neurotrophic factor (BDNF) and stimulate the mammalian target of rapamycin (mTOR) pathway, both of which are essential for neuroplasticity (Ly et al., 2018).

2. **Increased Dendritic Spine Density:** Dendritic spines are small protrusions on neurons that form synapses and facilitate communication between brain cells. Their density and structure are critical indicators of neuroplasticity.

• Psilocybin's Effect: Studies have shown that psilocybin increases dendritic spine density and size in the prefrontal cortex, enhancing synaptic strength and connectivity (Ly et al., 2018).

• Timeframe: These structural changes are observed within 24 hours of psilocybin administration and can persist for weeks, indicating long-lasting effects on brain plasticity.

3. **Enhanced Synaptogenesis:** Synaptogenesis, the formation of new synapses, is a fundamental aspect of neuroplasticity. Psilocybin facilitates synaptogenesis by promoting the release of growth factors like BDNF.

• BDNF's Role: BDNF supports the survival, growth, and differentiation of neurons and is critical for adapting to new learning and emotional challenges (Duman & Monteggia, 2006).

• Psilocybin's Impact: By increasing BDNF levels, psilocybin fosters the creation of new synaptic connections, particularly in areas involved in learning and emotional regulation.

4. **Modulation of Cortical Plasticity:** Psilocybin enhances cortical plasticity, allowing the brain to reorganize itself in response to external stimuli.

• Functional Connectivity: Functional magnetic resonance imaging (fMRI) studies reveal that psilocybin increases global brain connectivity, enabling regions that typically operate independently to communicate more effectively (Tagliazucchi et al., 2016).

• Breaking Rigid Patterns: This connectivity allows individuals to break free from rigid thought patterns, which is particularly beneficial for conditions like depression and PTSD.

Scientific Evidence of Psilocybin-Induced Neuroplasticity

1. **Structural Changes in Neurons:** Ly et al. (2018) demonstrated that psilocybin significantly increases the number of dendritic spines and synaptic connections in rodent models. These changes were accompanied by improved behavior in stress-related tasks, suggesting functional benefits of enhanced plasticity.

2. **Functional Brain Imaging:** Carhart-Harris et al. (2012) conducted fMRI studies showing that psilocybin alters the activity of brain networks, particularly the default mode network (DMN). These changes facilitate neuroplasticity by disrupting maladaptive neural circuits and encouraging new connections.

3. **Antidepressant Effects:** A clinical trial by Davis et al. (2020) found that psilocybin produced rapid and sustained antidepressant effects in patients with major depressive disorder. These effects were attributed to increased neuroplasticity, as evidenced by improved emotional flexibility and cognitive function.

4. **Persistence of Effects:** Research indicates that psilocybin-induced neuroplastic changes can persist for weeks or even months after administration, making it a promising tool for long-term mental health improvement (Madsen et al., 2019).

Applications of Psilocybin-Induced Neuroplasticity

1. **Treatment of Depression:** Depression is associated with reduced neuroplasticity and impaired synaptic connectivity. Psilocybin's ability to increase BDNF levels and promote synaptic growth offers a novel approach to restoring normal brain function (Ly et al., 2018).

   • Mechanism: By activating 5-HT2A receptors, psilocybin enhances neuroplasticity, allowing the brain to adapt to positive thought patterns and reduce depressive symptoms.

2. **PTSD and Trauma Recovery:** Trauma disrupts neural circuits involved in emotional regulation. Psilocybin helps reorganize these circuits by promoting neuroplasticity and enhancing emotional resilience.

   • Evidence: Studies in rodent models show that psilocybin reduces fear responses and facilitates the extinction of trauma-related memories, a process dependent on plasticity (Nichols, 2016).

3. **Addiction Treatment:** Addiction involves rigid neural pathways that reinforce compulsive behaviors. Psilocybin's ability to increase neuroplasticity helps individuals develop new coping strategies and break free from addictive patterns.

- Clinical Insights: Psilocybin-assisted therapy has shown promise in treating alcohol and nicotine addiction, with long-term abstinence rates linked to enhanced brain connectivity (Bogenschutz et al., 2015).

Scientific Facts About Psilocybin and Neuroplasticity

1. Psilocybin increases dendritic spine density. These changes are observable within 24 hours and persist for weeks (Ly et al., 2018).

2. Psilocybin promotes synaptogenesis. This effect is mediated by the release of BDNF and activation of the mTOR pathway.

3. Activation of 5-HT2A receptors is critical for neuroplasticity. These receptors regulate synaptic growth and cortical reorganization (Nichols, 2016).

4. Psilocybin enhances global brain connectivity. Increased communication between brain regions supports adaptive learning and emotional flexibility (Tagliazucchi et al., 2016).

5. Neuroplastic changes correlate with therapeutic benefits. Patients with increased neuroplasticity show greater improvements in depression, anxiety, and PTSD symptoms (Davis et al., 2020).

6. Psilocybin's effects on neuroplasticity are dose-dependent. Even microdoses can promote subtle changes in plasticity, contributing to mood and cognitive improvements.

7. Psilocybin reduces DMN activity. This disruption allows for the formation of new neural pathways and perspectives (Carhart-Harris et al., 2012).

8. BDNF levels increase after psilocybin administration. Elevated BDNF supports neuronal growth and resilience (Duman & Monteggia, 2006).

9. Psilocybin reverses stress-induced neuronal atrophy. This effect has been observed in preclinical studies, highlighting its potential for treating chronic stress-related disorders.

10. Psilocybin facilitates emotional learning. Enhanced plasticity allows for the rewiring of maladaptive emotional responses, such as those seen in trauma or anxiety disorders.

Conclusion

Psilocybin's ability to increase neuroplasticity is a key factor underlying its therapeutic potential. By promoting synaptic growth, enhancing brain connectivity, and increasing the availability of growth factors like BDNF, psilocybin facilitates the reorganization of neural pathways that govern mood, cognition, and behavior. These effects make it a promising tool for treating a range of mental health conditions, from depression and anxiety to PTSD and addiction. As research continues, understanding the mechanisms of psilocybin-induced neuroplasticity will pave the way for its integration into modern psychiatric practice.

References

1. Ly, C., et al. (2018). "Psychedelics promote structural and functional neural plasticity."

2. Carhart-Harris, R. L., et al. (2012). "Neural correlates of the psychedelic state as determined by fMRI studies with psilocybin."

3. Nichols, D. E. (2016). "Psychedelics: Mechanisms of action and therapeutic potential."

4. Tagliazucchi, E., et al. (2016). "Increased global brain connectivity under psilocybin."

5. Davis, A. K., et al. (2020). "Effects of psilocybin-assisted therapy on major depressive disorder: A randomized clinical trial."

6. Duman, R. S., & Monteggia, L. M. (2006). "A neurotrophic model for stress-related mood disorders."

7. Bogenschutz, M. P., et al. (2015). "Psilocybin-assisted treatment for alcohol dependence: A proof-of-concept study."

Elevate Brain-Derived Neurotrophic Factor (BDNF) Levels

Brain-Derived Neurotrophic Factor (BDNF) is a critical protein involved in neuroplasticity, synaptic connectivity, and neuronal survival. Psilocybin mushrooms, through their active compound psilocin, have been shown to elevate BDNF levels, contributing to their profound therapeutic effects on mood, cognition, and mental health disorders. This chapter explores the mechanisms by which psilocybin influences BDNF, the role of BDNF in brain function, and the therapeutic implications of this interaction.

What is Brain-Derived Neurotrophic Factor (BDNF)?

BDNF is a neurotrophin, a class of proteins that support the survival, growth, and differentiation of neurons in the brain. It plays a key role in:

•	Neuroplasticity: Facilitating the formation and strengthening of synaptic connections.

•	Memory and Learning: Enhancing the hippocampus's ability to process and store information.

•	Mood Regulation: Supporting neural adaptability to environmental and emotional changes.

Low levels of BDNF have been implicated in several mental health disorders, including depression, anxiety, and PTSD (Duman & Monteggia, 2006). Thus, strategies to elevate BDNF are of great interest in psychiatric research.

How Psilocybin Elevates BDNF Levels

1. **Activation of Serotonin Receptors:** The elevation of BDNF by psilocybin is mediated through its active metabolite, psilocin, which binds to serotonin (5-HT) receptors.

• 5-HT2A Receptor Activation: Psilocin acts as a partial agonist at 5-HT2A receptors, triggering a cascade of intracellular signaling pathways that lead to increased BDNF expression. These receptors are abundant in the prefrontal cortex and hippocampus, regions critical for cognition and emotional regulation (Ly et al., 2018).

• Downstream Pathways: Activation of 5-HT2A receptors stimulates the release of calcium ions and activates the mitogen-activated protein kinase (MAPK) and mammalian target of rapamycin (mTOR) pathways, both of which are essential for BDNF synthesis (Nichols, 2016).

2. **Promotion of Synaptic Plasticity:** By enhancing BDNF levels, psilocybin supports synaptic plasticity, the brain's ability to adapt by forming new neural connections.

• Dendritic Growth: BDNF promotes the growth and branching of dendrites, the structures that allow neurons to communicate. Psilocybin's effects on BDNF contribute to increased dendritic spine density and improved synaptic strength (Ly et al., 2018).

• Long-Term Potentiation (LTP): Elevated BDNF levels enhance LTP, a process that strengthens synapses in response to repeated stimulation, which is essential for learning and memory.

3. **Reduction of Neuroinflammation:** Psilocybin reduces neuroinflammation, which can suppress BDNF production.

• Anti-Inflammatory Effects: Psilocybin decreases levels of pro-inflammatory cytokines, such as interleukin-6 (IL-6) and tumor necrosis factor-alpha (TNF-α). Reduced inflammation creates a favorable environment for BDNF synthesis (Ly et al., 2018).

4. **Stress Reduction and HPA Axis Modulation:** Chronic stress and dysregulation of the hypothalamic-pituitary-adrenal (HPA) axis are associated with decreased BDNF levels. Psilocybin mitigates these effects.

• Stress Resilience: Psilocybin normalizes HPA axis activity, reducing cortisol levels and protecting neurons from stress-induced damage. This stabilization supports BDNF expression and neurogenesis.

Therapeutic Implications of Elevated BDNF

1. **Depression:** Low BDNF levels are a hallmark of depression. Psilocybin's ability to elevate BDNF provides a biological basis for its rapid and sustained antidepressant effects.

• Clinical Evidence: Davis et al. (2020) conducted a randomized controlled trial showing that a single psilocybin session produced significant and long-lasting reductions in depressive symptoms. These effects were attributed to enhanced neuroplasticity driven by elevated BDNF levels.

• Mechanism: Increased BDNF levels promote the formation of new neural pathways, helping patients adopt more adaptive thought patterns and emotional responses.

2. **Anxiety and PTSD:** Elevated BDNF helps rewire fear and anxiety circuits, facilitating emotional resilience and recovery from trauma.

• Fear Extinction: Psilocybin enhances fear extinction, a process dependent on BDNF. This effect is particularly beneficial for individuals with PTSD, as it allows them to process and move past traumatic memories (Nichols, 2016).

• Amygdala Regulation: BDNF supports the functional integration of the amygdala and prefrontal cortex, helping regulate fear responses.

3. **Addiction Treatment:** Addiction is associated with maladaptive neural circuits that reinforce compulsive behaviors. Elevated BDNF levels enable the brain to form new, healthier connections.

• Clinical Applications: Psilocybin has shown promise in treating substance use disorders, such as alcohol and nicotine addiction. Enhanced BDNF levels likely play a role by facilitating neural reorganization and improving cognitive flexibility (Bogenschutz et al., 2015).

4. **Cognitive Enhancement:** BDNF is essential for learning and memory, making its elevation a potential strategy for cognitive enhancement.

• Hippocampal Plasticity: Increased BDNF levels improve hippocampal function, enhancing memory consolidation and retrieval. Psilocybin's effects on BDNF may benefit conditions like age-related cognitive decline and Alzheimer's disease (Ly et al., 2018).

Scientific Evidence Supporting Psilocybin's Role in Elevating BDNF

1. **Preclinical Studies:** Ly et al. (2018) demonstrated that psilocybin significantly increased BDNF expression in rodent models. These changes were accompanied by enhanced dendritic growth and improved stress resilience.

2. **Functional Imaging:** Carhart-Harris et al. (2012) used fMRI to show that psilocybin promotes functional reorganization of brain networks, a process dependent on BDNF-mediated plasticity.

3. **Human Trials:** Davis et al. (2020) observed sustained antidepressant effects following psilocybin therapy, correlating with markers of increased neuroplasticity, such as elevated BDNF levels.

4. **Cellular Mechanisms:** Studies have shown that activation of the mTOR pathway by psilocin enhances BDNF synthesis, supporting synaptic growth and repair (Nichols, 2016).

Scientific Facts About Psilocybin and BDNF Elevation

1. Psilocybin increases BDNF levels through 5-HT2A receptor activation. These receptors are critical for initiating intracellular pathways that promote BDNF synthesis (Ly et al., 2018).

2. Elevated BDNF supports synaptic plasticity. This effect underlies psilocybin's ability to improve mood, cognition, and emotional regulation.

3. Psilocybin promotes dendritic growth. Increased BDNF levels lead to enhanced dendritic spine density and synaptic connectivity.

4. BDNF elevation correlates with therapeutic outcomes. Patients with increased BDNF levels show greater improvements in depression, anxiety, and PTSD (Davis et al., 2020).

5. Psilocybin reduces neuroinflammation. Anti-inflammatory effects create a favorable environment for BDNF expression.

6. BDNF elevation enhances fear extinction. This mechanism helps individuals overcome trauma and anxiety disorders.

7. BDNF plays a role in addiction recovery. Elevated levels facilitate the rewiring of maladaptive neural circuits.

8. Psilocybin's effects on BDNF are long-lasting. Elevated BDNF levels persist after the acute psychedelic experience, supporting sustained therapeutic benefits.

Conclusion

Psilocybin mushrooms elevate brain-derived neurotrophic factor (BDNF) levels, enhancing neuroplasticity, synaptic connectivity, and neuronal resilience. This effect underpins psilocybin's therapeutic potential for treating depression, anxiety, PTSD, and addiction while also offering benefits for cognitive enhancement. By activating serotonin receptors and downstream signaling pathways, psilocybin creates a favorable environment for neural growth and repair. As research continues, understanding the role of BDNF in psilocybin's effects will further clarify its mechanisms and therapeutic applications.

References

1. Ly, C., et al. (2018). "Psychedelics promote structural and functional neural plasticity."

2. Carhart-Harris, R. L., et al. (2012). "Neural correlates of the psychedelic state as determined by fMRI studies with psilocybin."

3.   Nichols, D. E. (2016). "Psychedelics: Mechanisms of action and therapeutic potential."

4.   Davis, A. K., et al. (2020). "Effects of psilocybin-assisted therapy on major depressive disorder: A randomized clinical trial."

5.   Bogenschutz, M. P., et al. (2015). "Psilocybin-assisted treatment for alcohol dependence: A proof-of-concept study."

6.   Duman, R. S., & Monteggia, L. M. (2006). "A neurotrophic model for stress-related mood disorders."

Reducing Default Mode Network (DMN) Activity

Psilocybin mushrooms have gained significant attention for their ability to modulate brain activity, particularly in the Default Mode Network (DMN). The DMN, a network of interconnected brain regions active during self-referential thinking and mind-wandering, plays a central role in maintaining our sense of self and processing internal thoughts. Overactivity in the DMN is associated with mental health conditions like depression, anxiety, and rumination. This chapter explores how psilocybin mushrooms reduce DMN activity, the mechanisms involved, and the therapeutic implications, supported by scientific evidence.

What is the Default Mode Network?

The Default Mode Network (DMN) comprises several brain regions, including:

1.   **Medial Prefrontal Cortex (mPFC)**: Associated with self-referential thought, such as reflecting on personal experiences.

2.   **Posterior Cingulate Cortex (PCC)**: Involved in memory and the integration of information about the self and the environment.

3.   **Precuneus**: Plays a role in consciousness and self-awareness.

4.   **Angular Gyrus**: Related to processing of language and abstract thought.

DMN's Role in Mental Health

•   Overactivity in the DMN is linked to excessive self-focus, rumination, and negative thought patterns, characteristic of depression and anxiety.

•   An imbalance between the DMN and task-positive networks (involved in external attention) can lead to cognitive rigidity and emotional dysregulation.

Psilocybin's Effects on the DMN

1. **Disruption of DMN Connectivity:** Psilocybin reduces the functional connectivity within the DMN. This effect has been observed using functional magnetic resonance imaging (fMRI) and magnetoencephalography (MEG).

•   Scientific Findings: Carhart-Harris et al. (2012) demonstrated that psilocybin decreases activity in the mPFC and PCC, key nodes of the DMN. This reduction was associated with ego dissolution, a phenomenon where individuals experience a loss of self-boundaries and feel a sense of unity with their surroundings.

2. **Functional Reorganization:** Psilocybin promotes increased communication between the DMN and other brain networks, such as the salience network and task-positive network.

•   Enhanced Brain Connectivity: Studies reveal that psilocybin increases global brain connectivity, allowing for greater interaction between typically segregated regions (Tagliazucchi et al., 2016). This reorganization enables new patterns of thought and behavior, breaking the repetitive loops often associated with mental health conditions.

Mechanisms Behind DMN Reduction

1. **5-HT2A Receptor Activation:** The primary mechanism through which psilocybin reduces DMN activity is its action on serotonin 5-HT2A receptors.

•   Location: These receptors are densely located in the cortical regions that form the DMN, including the mPFC and PCC.

•   Impact: Activation of 5-HT2A receptors disrupts synchronized DMN activity, facilitating the breakdown of rigid self-referential thought patterns (Nichols, 2016).

2. **Alterations in Oscillatory Activity:** Psilocybin induces changes in brainwave activity, particularly in alpha and gamma oscillations, which are closely tied to DMN function.

•   Alpha Oscillations: Psilocybin decreases alpha power, particularly in the PCC, which correlates with reduced DMN activity and ego dissolution (Muthukumaraswamy et al., 2013).

- Gamma Oscillations: Increased gamma activity under psilocybin reflects heightened integration of sensory and cognitive processes, promoting a more flexible and interconnected brain state.

Therapeutic Implications of DMN Reduction
1. Depression and Rumination

- DMN Overactivity in Depression: Depression is associated with hyperactivity in the DMN, leading to persistent negative thoughts and self-criticism.

- Psilocybin's Role: By reducing DMN activity, psilocybin disrupts these maladaptive thought patterns, allowing individuals to adopt new perspectives. Carhart-Harris et al. (2017) found that psilocybin therapy led to significant reductions in depressive symptoms, correlated with DMN modulation.

2. Anxiety Disorders

- Role of DMN: Overactive DMN regions contribute to excessive worry and heightened self-awareness in anxiety disorders.

- Psilocybin Therapy: Studies have shown that psilocybin reduces DMN hyperconnectivity, promoting relaxation and a sense of detachment from anxiety-provoking thoughts (Griffiths et al., 2016).

3. Addiction

- Behavioral Rigidity in Addiction: Addictive behaviors are often driven by rigid neural circuits involving the DMN.

- Breaking Addictive Patterns: Psilocybin's ability to reduce DMN activity and enhance brain connectivity helps disrupt these circuits, enabling individuals to develop healthier coping mechanisms (Bogenschutz et al., 2015).

Scientific Evidence Supporting DMN Reduction
1. **Functional Imaging Studies:** Carhart-Harris et al. (2012) conducted an fMRI study showing that psilocybin significantly reduces blood flow to DMN hubs, particularly the mPFC and PCC. Participants reported profound ego dissolution, which was directly linked to decreased DMN activity.

2. **MEG Studies:** Muthukumaraswamy et al. (2013) used MEG to demonstrate reductions in alpha power in the PCC under psilocybin. This change was associated with altered states of consciousness and reduced self-referential processing.

3. **Long-Term Effects:** Psilocybin's effects on the DMN persist long after the acute experience. Carhart-Harris et al. (2017) found that patients with treatment-resistant depression showed sustained improvements in mood weeks after a single psilocybin session, with DMN changes correlating with these outcomes.

Scientific Facts About Psilocybin and DMN Modulation

1. Psilocybin reduces connectivity within the DMN. This disruption correlates with ego dissolution and therapeutic effects (Carhart-Harris et al., 2012).

2. DMN reduction is mediated by 5-HT2A receptor activation. These receptors are abundant in cortical areas forming the DMN (Nichols, 2016).

3. Psilocybin decreases alpha oscillations in DMN hubs. Reduced alpha power is associated with altered self-perception and increased emotional openness (Muthukumaraswamy et al., 2013).

4. Increased global connectivity complements DMN reduction. Psilocybin enhances interactions between the DMN and other brain networks, promoting cognitive flexibility (Tagliazucchi et al., 2016).

5. DMN activity normalizes after psilocybin therapy. Sustained changes in DMN connectivity are linked to long-term improvements in depression and anxiety (Carhart-Harris et al., 2017).

6. DMN suppression allows for reorganization of brain activity. This effect underpins psilocybin's ability to break maladaptive thought loops (Griffiths et al., 2016).

7. DMN modulation is dose-dependent. Higher doses of psilocybin lead to more pronounced reductions in DMN activity.

Conclusion

Psilocybin mushrooms reduce activity in the Default Mode Network, facilitating a breakdown of rigid self-referential thinking and promoting greater connectivity between brain regions. This disruption is central to psilocybin's therapeutic effects, enabling individuals to overcome conditions like depression, anxiety, and addiction. By altering DMN activity through serotonin receptor activation and changes in brainwave patterns, psilocybin fosters cognitive flexibility and emotional resilience. As research continues, DMN modulation remains a key focus in understanding and leveraging psilocybin's potential in mental health treatment.

References

1. Carhart-Harris, R. L., et al. (2012). "Neural correlates of the psychedelic state as determined by fMRI studies with psilocybin."

2. Muthukumaraswamy, S. D., et al. (2013). "Enhanced alpha power during resting state under psilocybin."

3. Tagliazucchi, E., et al. (2016). "Increased global brain connectivity under psilocybin."

4. Carhart-Harris, R. L., et al. (2017). "Psilocybin with psychological support for treatment-resistant depression: six-month follow-up."

5. Nichols, D. E. (2016). "Psychedelics: Mechanisms of action and therapeutic potential."

6. Griffiths, R. R., et al. (2016). "Psilocybin produces substantial and sustained decreases in depression and anxiety in patients with life-threatening cancer."

7. Bogenschutz, M. P., et al. (2015). "Psilocybin-assisted treatment for alcohol dependence: A proof-of-concept study."

Increases Glutamate Levels

Psilocin, the active metabolite of psilocybin, interacts with multiple neurotransmitter systems in the brain, one of the most critical being the glutamatergic system. Glutamate is the brain's primary excitatory neurotransmitter, essential for synaptic plasticity, learning, memory, and cognitive flexibility. By increasing glutamate levels, psilocin facilitates neuroplasticity and reorganization of neural circuits, underpinning its therapeutic effects for mental health conditions such as depression, anxiety, and PTSD. This chapter explores the mechanisms by which psilocin elevates glutamate, its downstream effects, and its implications for neuroscience and psychiatry.

The Role of Glutamate in Brain Function

Glutamate is the most abundant excitatory neurotransmitter in the brain, playing a vital role in:

1. **Synaptic Plasticity**: Modifying the strength of synaptic connections in response to experience or learning.

2. **Memory and Learning**: Facilitating long-term potentiation (LTP), a cellular process underlying memory formation.

3. **Neurotransmission**: Mediating communication between neurons in key brain regions, such as the prefrontal cortex and hippocampus.

Abnormalities in glutamate signaling are implicated in several psychiatric disorders. For example:

•   **Depression**: Reduced glutamate activity and impaired plasticity in the prefrontal cortex and hippocampus.

•   **PTSD**: Dysfunctional glutamate signaling leads to hyperactive fear responses.

•   **Addiction**: Imbalanced glutamate pathways perpetuate maladaptive behaviors.

How Psilocin Elevates Glutamate Levels

1. **Activation of 5-HT2A Receptors:** The primary mechanism by which psilocin increases glutamate levels is through its action on serotonin (5-HT) receptors, particularly the 5-HT2A subtype.

 • Receptor Localization: 5-HT2A receptors are densely expressed on pyramidal neurons in the prefrontal cortex, a region crucial for executive function, emotional regulation, and decision-making (Nichols, 2016).

 • Neuronal Excitation: Activation of 5-HT2A receptors by psilocin enhances excitatory neurotransmission in these neurons, leading to increased release of glutamate into the synaptic cleft (Muller et al., 2018).

 • Downstream Signaling: The release of glutamate triggers activation of ionotropic glutamate receptors (AMPA and NMDA receptors) on postsynaptic neurons, enhancing synaptic plasticity and neural connectivity.

2. **Modulation of Cortical Networks:** Psilocin-induced glutamate release modulates activity across cortical networks, promoting integration and flexibility.

 • Increased Pyramidal Neuron Activity: By exciting pyramidal neurons in the prefrontal cortex, psilocin amplifies glutamate signaling, enhancing top-down control over other brain regions (Carhart-Harris et al., 2012).

 • Feedback Loops: Glutamate release creates positive feedback loops that further activate serotonergic and dopaminergic systems, contributing to the subjective effects of psilocybin, such as enhanced cognition and emotional insights.

3. **Enhanced Glutamate-GABA Balance:** Psilocin's effects on glutamate also influence gamma-aminobutyric acid (GABA), the brain's primary inhibitory neurotransmitter. Maintaining a balance between glutamate and GABA is essential for healthy neural function.

 • Glutamate and GABA Interplay: Elevated glutamate levels indirectly regulate GABAergic interneurons, ensuring balanced excitation and inhibition across neural circuits. This balance prevents overstimulation and supports stable cognitive and emotional states.

Therapeutic Implications of Elevated Glutamate

1. **Depression:** Low glutamate activity in the prefrontal cortex and hippocampus is a hallmark of depression. Psilocin's ability to increase glutamate levels provides a mechanistic basis for its rapid and sustained antidepressant effects.

   • Neuroplasticity: Elevated glutamate levels enhance synaptic plasticity, enabling the brain to form new neural pathways and adopt healthier thought patterns.

   • Clinical Evidence: A study by Davis et al. (2020) found that psilocybin therapy significantly improved depressive symptoms, with increased glutamate signaling implicated as a key factor.

2. **Anxiety and PTSD:** By increasing glutamate, psilocin helps rewire neural circuits involved in fear and anxiety responses.

   • Fear Extinction: Elevated glutamate levels facilitate fear extinction, a process mediated by NMDA receptor activity. This effect is particularly beneficial for patients with PTSD, allowing them to process and move beyond traumatic memories (Nichols, 2016).

   • Amygdala Regulation: Glutamate signaling supports the functional integration of the amygdala and prefrontal cortex, helping regulate emotional responses.

3. **Addiction Recovery:** Addiction is characterized by disrupted glutamate pathways that reinforce maladaptive behaviors. Psilocin's effects on glutamate enable the brain to reorganize these pathways.

  • Neural Reorganization: Elevated glutamate levels promote neuroplasticity, allowing individuals to break free from addictive patterns.

  • Clinical Applications: Psilocybin-assisted therapy has shown promise in treating addiction to alcohol, nicotine, and other substances, with glutamate signaling playing a pivotal role (Bogenschutz et al., 2015).

4. **Cognitive Enhancement:** Glutamate is essential for learning, memory, and cognitive flexibility. Psilocin's effects on glutamate make it a promising tool for cognitive enhancement and neuroprotection.

  • Hippocampal Function: Increased glutamate levels enhance memory formation and retrieval by supporting long-term potentiation in the hippocampus.

  • Applications: Psilocin's ability to boost glutamate signaling may benefit conditions such as age-related cognitive decline and Alzheimer's disease (Ly et al., 2018).

Scientific Evidence Supporting Psilocin's Role in Glutamate Modulation

1. **Preclinical Studies:** Muller et al. (2018) demonstrated that psilocybin increases glutamate levels in the prefrontal cortex of rodent models. These changes were associated with enhanced synaptic plasticity and stress resilience.

2. **Functional Imaging:** Carhart-Harris et al. (2012) used fMRI to show that psilocybin modulates cortical activity, particularly in the prefrontal cortex, a process dependent on glutamate signaling.

3. **Clinical Trials:** Davis et al. (2020) observed significant improvements in mood and cognition following psilocybin therapy, correlating with increased glutamate activity in key brain regions.

4. **Molecular Mechanisms:** Activation of AMPA and NMDA receptors by glutamate enhances neuroplasticity and supports therapeutic outcomes, as demonstrated in studies on psilocybin's effects on neural circuits (Nichols, 2016).

Scientific Facts About Psilocin and Glutamate

1. Psilocin increases glutamate release through 5-HT2A receptor activation. These receptors are abundant in pyramidal neurons in the prefrontal cortex (Nichols, 2016).

2. Elevated glutamate enhances synaptic plasticity. This effect underlies psilocybin's ability to improve mood, cognition, and emotional regulation (Ly et al., 2018).

3. Glutamate facilitates fear extinction. NMDA receptor activation by glutamate supports the reorganization of fear circuits in PTSD (Nichols, 2016).

4. Glutamate modulates cortical networks. Increased glutamate activity enhances functional connectivity between brain regions (Carhart-Harris et al., 2012).

5. Glutamate signaling correlates with therapeutic outcomes. Elevated glutamate levels are associated with reductions in depression, anxiety, and addictive behaviors (Davis et al., 2020).

6. Psilocybin improves glutamate-GABA balance. This interplay ensures stable neural activity and prevents overstimulation.

7. Psilocin's effects on glutamate are dose-dependent. Higher doses produce more pronounced increases in glutamate activity.

8. Glutamate boosts cognitive flexibility. Psilocin's effects on glutamate improve problem-solving and creative thinking.

Conclusion

Psilocin, the active metabolite of psilocybin, increases glutamate levels in key brain regions, facilitating neuroplasticity, synaptic connectivity, and cognitive flexibility. By modulating the glutamatergic system, psilocin promotes emotional resilience, cognitive enhancement, and recovery from mental health conditions like depression, PTSD, and addiction. These effects highlight the potential of psilocybin mushrooms as a powerful tool in neuroscience and psychiatry. Continued research into psilocin's effects on glutamate will further clarify its mechanisms and expand its therapeutic applications.

References

1.	Nichols, D. E. (2016). "Psychedelics: Mechanisms of action and therapeutic potential."

2.	Muller, F., et al. (2018). "The therapeutic potential of psilocybin for psychiatric disorders: A review."

3.	Carhart-Harris, R. L., et al. (2012). "Neural correlates of the psychedelic state as determined by fMRI studies with psilocybin."

4.	Davis, A. K., et al. (2020). "Effects of psilocybin-assisted therapy on major depressive disorder: A randomized clinical trial."

5.	Ly, C., et al. (2018). "Psychedelics promote structural and functional neural plasticity."

6.	Bogenschutz, M. P., et al. (2015). "Psilocybin-assisted treatment for alcohol dependence: A proof-of-concept study."

Conclusions

Psilocybin mushrooms represent a remarkable avenue in neuroscience and psychiatry, offering profound effects on brain function and promising therapeutic applications. Through their active compound, psilocybin, these mushrooms influence a variety of neurochemical and physiological processes, leading to significant benefits for mental health. Below, we consolidate the key findings from scientific studies on psilocybin's mechanisms of action, therapeutic potential, and unique characteristics.

1. Mechanisms of Action
1.1 Interaction with Serotonin Receptors

Psilocybin exerts its effects primarily by activating serotonin (5-HT) receptors, particularly the 5-HT2A subtype. This receptor activity enhances excitatory neurotransmission, modulates mood and cognition, and triggers downstream processes like neuroplasticity and emotional regulation (Nichols, 2016; Madsen et al., 2019). Unlike substances targeting the dopamine system, psilocybin's action on serotonin receptors minimizes the risk of addiction and physical dependence.

1.2 Enhanced Neuroplasticity

Psilocybin promotes the growth of dendritic spines, synaptic connections, and neurogenesis in key brain regions like the prefrontal cortex and hippocampus. These changes, mediated by increased levels of brain-derived neurotrophic factor (BDNF), enable the brain to reorganize maladaptive neural circuits, making it a promising treatment for depression, anxiety, PTSD, and addiction (Ly et al., 2018; Davis et al., 2020).

1.3 Glutamate Modulation

By enhancing glutamate release, psilocybin strengthens synaptic connectivity and fosters cognitive flexibility. This action supports its therapeutic effects on learning, memory, and emotional resilience (Muller et al., 2018).

1.4 Anti-Inflammatory Effects
Psilocybin reduces levels of pro-inflammatory cytokines like interleukin-6 (IL-6) and tumor necrosis factor-alpha (TNF-α), while promoting the release of anti-inflammatory molecules like interleukin-10 (IL-10). This dual action mitigates neuroinflammation, a key contributor to depression, anxiety, and neurodegenerative diseases (Nichols, 2016; Ly et al., 2018).

1.5 Alteration of Brainwave Activity
Psilocybin induces profound changes in brainwave dynamics, including the suppression of alpha waves, elevation of gamma oscillations, and enhancement of theta activity. These changes disrupt rigid patterns of self-referential thinking and facilitate emotional breakthroughs and cognitive flexibility (Muthukumaraswamy et al., 2013; Carhart-Harris et al., 2014).

2. Therapeutic Applications
2.1 Depression
Psilocybin demonstrates rapid and sustained antidepressant effects, even in cases of treatment-resistant depression. Its ability to disrupt overactive default mode network (DMN) activity, elevate BDNF levels, and enhance neuroplasticity enables patients to adopt healthier thought patterns (Carhart-Harris et al., 2016; Davis et al., 2020).

2.2 Anxiety and PTSD
By modulating the amygdala and promoting fear extinction through increased glutamate and theta activity, psilocybin helps patients process traumatic memories and reduce anxiety (Nichols, 2016; Roseman et al., 2017).

2.3 Addiction
Psilocybin's ability to reorganize neural circuits involved in reward processing and compulsive behaviors makes it a promising tool for treating substance use disorders.

Clinical studies have shown significant reductions in alcohol and nicotine dependence with psilocybin-assisted therapy (Bogenschutz et al., 2015).

2.4 Cognitive Enhancement

Through enhanced gamma oscillations and synaptic growth, psilocybin promotes creativity, problem-solving, and memory formation. These effects may also benefit individuals with age-related cognitive decline or neurodegenerative diseases (Tagliazucchi et al., 2016; Ly et al., 2018).

3. Unique Characteristics
3.1 Lack of Physical Dependence

Unlike many psychoactive substances, psilocybin does not induce physical dependence or withdrawal symptoms. Its action on serotonin rather than dopamine pathways, combined with its introspective and self-regulating nature, minimizes the risk of misuse (Nichols, 2016; Halberstadt & Geyer, 2011).

3.2 Rapid and Long-Lasting Effects

Psilocybin produces therapeutic benefits within hours of administration, with effects lasting for weeks or months. This rapid onset and sustained impact make it a valuable alternative to conventional antidepressants and anxiolytics (Carhart-Harris et al., 2017).

3.3 Non-Compulsive Use Patterns

Psilocybin's profound and emotionally taxing effects naturally discourage frequent use, aligning it well with structured therapeutic protocols.

Conclusion

Psilocybin mushrooms represent a paradigm shift in mental health treatment, offering rapid, sustained, and safe therapeutic benefits for a range of conditions. By enhancing neuroplasticity, modulating brainwave activity, reducing inflammation, and promoting emotional breakthroughs, psilocybin addresses the root causes of psychiatric disorders. Its lack of physical dependence and unique mechanisms of action further underscore its potential as a transformative tool in psychiatry and neuroscience.

As research continues, psilocybin's integration into clinical practice may redefine approaches to mental health care, providing relief for millions suffering from depression, anxiety, PTSD, addiction, and other conditions.

References

1. Nichols, D. E. (2016). "Psychedelics: Mechanisms of action and therapeutic potential."

2. Ly, C., et al. (2018). "Psychedelics promote structural and functional neural plasticity."

3. Carhart-Harris, R. L., et al. (2012). "Neural correlates of the psychedelic state as determined by fMRI studies with psilocybin."

4. Davis, A. K., et al. (2020). "Effects of psilocybin-assisted therapy on major depressive disorder: A randomized clinical trial."

5. Muthukumaraswamy, S. D., et al. (2013). "Enhanced gamma oscillations and reduced alpha power under psilocybin."

6. Roseman, L., et al. (2017). "Increased amygdala responses to emotional faces after psilocybin therapy."

7. Bogenschutz, M. P., et al. (2015). "Psilocybin-assisted treatment for alcohol dependence: A proof-of-concept study."

8. Halberstadt, A. L., & Geyer, M. A. (2011). "Serotonergic hallucinogens as translational models relevant to schizophrenia."

9. Tagliazucchi, E., et al. (2016). "Increased global brain connectivity under psilocybin."

10. Carhart-Harris, R. L., et al. (2017). "Psilocybin with psychological support for treatment-resistant depression: six-month follow-up."

Made in the USA
Monee, IL
09 February 2025